This revised edition of JP 2-0, *Joint Intelligence*, reflects the current guidance for conducting joint and multinational intelligence activities across the range of military operations. This vital keystone publication forms the core of joint intelligence doctrine and lays the foundation for our forces' ability to fully integrate operations, plans, and intelligence into a cohesive team. The overarching constructs and principles contained in this publication provide a common perspective from which to plan and execute joint intelligence operations in cooperation with our multinational partners, other US Government agencies, and intergovernmental and nongovernmental organizations.

As our Nation continues into the 21st century, joint intelligence organizations and capabilities will continue to evolve as our forces transform to meet emerging challenges. The guidance in this publication will enable current and future leaders of the Armed Forces of the United States to organize, train, and execute worldwide missions to counter the threats posed by adaptive adversaries.

I encourage all leaders to study and understand the doctrinal concepts and principles contained in this publication and to teach these to your subordinates. Only then will we be able to fully exploit the remarkable military potential inherent in our joint teams. To that end, I request you ensure the widest possible distribution of this keystone joint publication. I further request that you actively promote the use of all joint publications at every opportunity.

MARTIN E. DEMPSEY
General, U.S. Army

PREFACE

1. Scope

This publication is the keystone document for joint intelligence. It provides fundamental principles and guidance for intelligence support to joint operations.

2. Purpose

This publication has been prepared under the direction of the Chairman of the Joint Chiefs of Staff (CJCS). It sets forth joint doctrine to govern the activities and performance of the Armed Forces of the United States in joint operations and provides the doctrinal basis for US military coordination with other US Government departments and agencies during operations and for US military involvement in multinational operations. It provides military guidance for the exercise of authority by combatant commanders and other joint force commanders (JFCs) and prescribes joint doctrine for operations, education, and training. It provides military guidance for use by the Armed Forces in preparing their appropriate plans. It is not the intent of this publication to restrict the authority of the JFC from organizing the force and executing the mission in a manner the JFC deems most appropriate to ensure unity of effort in the accomplishment of the overall objective.

3. Application

a. Joint doctrine established in this publication applies to the joint staff, commanders of combatant commands, subunified commands, joint task forces, subordinate components of these commands, the Services, and combat support agencies.

b. The guidance in this publication is authoritative; as such, this doctrine will be followed except when, in the judgment of the commander, exceptional circumstances dictate otherwise. If conflicts arise between the contents of this publication and the contents of Service publications, this publication will take precedence unless the CJCS, normally in coordination with the other members of the Joint Chiefs of Staff, has provided more current and specific guidance. Commanders of forces operating as part of a multinational (alliance or coalition) military command should follow multinational doctrine and procedures ratified by the United States. For doctrine and procedures not ratified by the United States, commanders should evaluate and follow the multinational command's doctrine and procedures, where applicable and consistent with US law, regulations, and doctrine.

Intentionally Blank

SUMMARY OF CHANGES
REVISION OF JOINT PUBLICATION 2-0
DATED 22 JUNE 2007

- Clarified the term "intelligence interrogation" and provided specific publications for guidance.

- Explained the joint intelligence process and rewrote the section to better develop its characteristics.

- Added the term "sociocultural analysis (SCA)." The phrase "other relevant actors" was included in the SCA explanation to cover not only direct adversaries, but any person or group that may aid the adversary.

- Added a description of "identity intelligence" and grouped it under production categories.

- Added the definition "collection strategy" and modified the terms "collection plan" and "collection requirement."

- Changed the term "indication and warning" to "warning" and modified the definition of "warning."

- Clarified the distinction between the term "red cell" and "red team."

Intentionally Blank

TABLE OF CONTENTS

Intentionally Blank

EXECUTIVE SUMMARY
COMMANDER'S OVERVIEW

- **Describes the Nature of Intelligence**

- **Presents the Principles of Joint Intelligence**

- **Describes Intelligence Organizations and Responsibilities**

- **Explains Intelligence Support to Planning, Executing, and Assessing Joint Operations**

- **Addresses Joint, Interagency, and Multinational Intelligence Sharing and Cooperation**

The Nature of Intelligence

Information on its own may be of utility to the commander, but when related to other information about the operational environment and considered in the light of past experience, it gives rise to a new understanding of the information, which may be termed "intelligence."

The management and integration of intelligence into military operations are inherent responsibilities of command. Information is of greatest value when it contributes to the commander's decision-making process by providing reasoned insight into future conditions or situations. Intelligence provides the commander a variety of assessments and estimates that facilitate understanding the operational environment (OE). Intelligence includes the organizations, capabilities, and processes involved in the collection, processing, exploitation, analysis, and dissemination of information or finished intelligence. Intelligence products provide users with the information that has been collected and analyzed based on their requirements.

The Roles and Responsibilities of Joint Intelligence

The primary role of joint intelligence is to provide information and assessments to facilitate mission accomplishment. This role is supported by a series of specific responsibilities to guide the intelligence directorate of a joint staff (J-2) and supporting organizations. These include: inform the commander, describe the OE; identify, define, and nominate objectives; support planning and execution of operations; counter adversary deception and surprise; support friendly deception efforts; and assess the effectiveness of operations.

The Joint Intelligence Process

The joint intelligence process provides the basis for common intelligence terminology and procedures. It consists of six interrelated categories of intelligence operations characterized by broad activities conducted by intelligence staffs and organizations for the purpose of providing commanders and national-level decision makers with relevant and timely intelligence. The six categories of intelligence operations are: planning and direction; collection; processing and exploitation; analysis and production; dissemination and integration; and evaluation and feedback. **Joint intelligence preparation of the operational environment (JIPOE)** is the continuous process through which J-2 manages the analysis and development of products that help the commander and staff understand the complex and interconnected OE—the composite of the conditions, circumstances, and influences that affect the employment of capabilities that bear on the decisions of the commander.

Intelligence and the Levels of War

...three levels of war: strategic, operational, and tactical...All levels of war have corresponding levels of intelligence operations.

Strategic Intelligence consist of the national strategic intelligence produced for the President, the National Security Council, Congress, Secretary of Defense (SecDef), senior military leaders, combatant commanders (CCDRs), and other US Government departments and agencies, and theater strategic intelligence that supports joint operations across the range of military operations, assesses the current situation, and estimates future capabilities and intentions of adversaries that could affect the national security and US or allied interests. **Operational intelligence** is primarily used by CCDRs and subordinate joint force commanders (JFCs) and their component commanders. **Tactical intelligence** is used by commanders, planners, and operators for planning and conducting battles, engagements, and special missions.

Principles of Joint Intelligence

Perspective

Intelligence analysts should strive to understand all relevant aspects of the OE. This understanding should include not only the adversary's disposition, but also the sociocultural nuances of individuals and groups in the OE.

Synchronization— (Synchronize Intelligence with Plans and Operations)

Intelligence should be synchronized with operations and plans in order to provide answers to intelligence requirements in time to influence the decision they are intended to support.

Integrity—(Remain Intellectually Honest)	Integrity requires adherence to facts and truthfulness with which those facts are interpreted and presented. Intelligence analysts should take active measures to recognize and avoid cognitive biases which affect their analysis.
Unity of Effort—(Cooperate to Achieve a Common Objective)	Unity of effort is facilitated by centralized planning and direction and decentralized execution of intelligence operations, which enables JFCs to apply all available collection capabilities and processing, exploitation, and dissemination systems, efficiently and effectively.
Prioritization—(Prioritize Requirements Based on Commander's Guidance)	Prioritization offers a mechanism for addressing requirements and effectively managing risk by identifying the most important tasks and applying available resources against those tasks.
Excellence—(Strive to Achieve the Highest Standards of Quality)	To achieve the highest standards of excellence, intelligence products must be: anticipatory, timely, accurate, usable, complete, relevant, objective, and available.
Prediction—(Accept the Risk of Predicting Adversary Intentions)	JFCs require and expect timely intelligence estimates that accurately identify adversary intentions, support offensive and/or defensive operations, and predict adversary future courses of action (COAs) in sufficient detail as to be actionable.
Agility—(Remain Flexible and Adapt to Changing Situations)	Agility is the ability to quickly shift focus and bring to bear the skill sets necessary to address the new problem at hand while simultaneously continuing critical preexisting work. Intelligence structures, methodologies, databases, products, and personnel should be sufficiently agile and flexible to meet changing operational situations, needs, priorities, and opportunities.
Collaboration—(Leverage Expertise of Diverse Analytic Resources)	By its nature intelligence is imperfect (i.e., everything cannot be known, analysis is vulnerable to deception, and information is open to alternative interpretations). The best way to avoid these obstacles and achieve a higher degree of fidelity is to consult with, and solicit the opinions of, other analysts and experts, particularly in external organizations.

Intelligence Organizations and Responsibilities

Defense Intelligence and the Intelligence Community

There are a variety of Department of Defense (DOD) and national intelligence organizations capable of providing support to joint operations. During most joint operations, JFCs will require federated support from the intelligence community (IC) to develop a full understanding of the OE. The **Director of National Intelligence (DNI)** has overall responsibility for intelligence support to the President and the day-to-day management of the IC. **Under Secretary of Defense for Intelligence (USD[I])** exercises SecDef's authority, direction, and control over the DOD agencies and DOD field activities that are defense intelligence, counterintelligence (CI), security, exercise, planning, policy, and strategic oversight over all DOD intelligence, CI, and security policy, plans, and programs. The **Director of the Defense Intelligence Agency (DIA)** advises SecDef and Deputy Secretary of Defense, Chairman of the Joint Chiefs of Staff (CJCS), CCDRs, and USD(I) on all matters concerning military and military-related intelligence and is the principal DOD intelligence representative in the national foreign intelligence process. Director DIA is the Defense Collection Manager; Commander, Joint Functional Component Command for Intelligence, Surveillance, and Reconnaissance (JFCC-ISR); Program Manager for the Joint Reserve Intelligence Program; Defense CI Manager; and Defense Human Intelligence Manager. The **Joint Staff Directorate for Intelligence, J-2**, provides continuous intelligence support to the CJCS, Joint Staff, National Military Command Center, and combatant commands (CCMDs) in the areas of targeting, global warning intelligence, and current intelligence. The J-2 also has the responsibility for coordinating the intelligence planning (IP) activities of the Services and intelligence combat support agencies (CSAs) in support of CCDRs. The **Service Chiefs**, their intelligence and CI chiefs, and staffs provide intelligence and CI support for departmental missions related to military systems, equipment, and training.

The intelligence community consists of the 17 member organizations (Defense Intelligence Agency, National Security Agency, National Geospatial Intelligence Agency, National Reconnaissance Office, Army Intelligence, Navy Intelligence, Air Force Intelligence, Marine Corps Intelligence, Central Intelligence Agency, Department of State, Department of Energy, Federal Bureau of Investigation, Department of the Treasury, Coast Guard Intelligence, Department of Homeland Security, the Drug Enforcement Administration, and the Office of Director of National Intelligence).

Defense and Joint Intelligence Organizations

In addition to the J-2 staffs at every joint level of command, the key organizations in the defense intelligence architecture are the CCMD joint intelligence operations centers (JIOCs), the joint task force (JTF) joint intelligence support elements (JISEs), JFCC-ISR, and the joint reserve intelligence centers (JRICs). At the JTF level, a JISE is normally established; however, a JIOC may be established at the direction of the JFC based on the scope, duration, and mission of the unit or JTF. The **National Joint Operations and Intelligence Center** is an integrated Joint Staff J-2/Operations Directorate/Plans Directorate element that monitors the global situation on a continual basis and provides the CJCS and SecDef a DOD planning and crisis response capability. The **CCMD JIOCs** are the primary intelligence organizations providing support to joint forces. The JIOC integrates the capabilities of DNI, Service, CSA, and CCMD intelligence assets to coordinate IP, collection management, analysis, and support. Under the direction of the joint force J-2, a JTF **JISE** normally manages the intelligence collection, production, analysis, and dissemination for a joint force. A **JRIC** is an intelligence production and training capability enabling Reserve Component intelligence forces to meet Service components, CCMDs, CSAs, and IC training, readiness, and operational requirements.

Intelligence Federation

Intelligence federation enables CCMDs to form support relationships with other theater JIOCs, Service intelligence centers, JRICs, or other DOD intelligence organizations to assist with the accomplishment of the joint force's mission. These support relationships, called federated partnerships, are preplanned agreements (formalized in operation plans [OPLANs], national intelligence support plans, or memorandums of agreement) intended to provide a rapid, flexible, surge capability enabling personnel from throughout the IC to assist the CCMD while remaining at their normal duty stations.

Command and Staff Intelligence Responsibilities

Commanders have key roles and responsibilities in the planning and conduct of intelligence operations. JFCs organize their joint force staff and assign responsibilities as necessary to ensure unity of effort and mission accomplishment. Commanders' intelligence responsibilities include: understand intelligence doctrine, capabilities, and limitations; provide planning guidance; define the area of interest (AOI); and specify intelligence priorities. The **J-2** assists the JFC in developing strategy, planning operations and campaigns, and tasking intelligence assets, for effective joint and multinational operations. Additionally, the J-2 is responsible for determining the requirements and direction needed to ensure unity of the intelligence effort and to support the commander's objectives. The **CCMD J-2** provides higher echelons and subordinate commands with a single, coordinated intelligence picture by fusing national and theater intelligence into all-source estimates and assessments.

Intelligence Support to Planning, Executing, and Assessing Joint Operations

Joint Operation Planning

During the joint operation planning process, CCMD J-2s lead development of annex B (Intelligence). Annex B is the intelligence annex to a plan or order that provides detailed information on the adversary situation, establishes priorities, assigns intelligence tasks, identifies required intelligence products, requests support from higher echelons, describes the concept of intelligence operations, and specifies intelligence procedures. The joint force J-2 products normally include but are not limited to the following: a description of the operational area; an evaluation of the adversary; identification of adversary centers of gravity; prioritized adversary COAs; event templates; named AOIs and target AOIs; a decision support template; wargame support; and an intelligence synchronization matrix.

The Intelligence Planning Process

IP activities are generally organized along two lines of effort (LOEs): providing intelligence support to joint operation planning and planning intelligence operations. **IP activities along the providing intelligence support to joint operation planning LOE** include the production of intelligence assessments and estimates of adversary intentions, capabilities, and COAs. Specific outputs of this LOE are the DIA-produced dynamic threat assessment, or theater intelligence assessment, and the development of tailored products from the CCMD's JIPOE process that culminate in the production and maintenance of the intelligence estimate. **IP activities along the planning intelligence operations LOE** include identifying information gaps, prioritizing intelligence requirements, developing federated production and integrated collection plans, and assessing intelligence capabilities for the purpose of identifying shortfalls and mitigation strategies. Specific outputs of this LOE are the CCMD J-2 staff estimate, which identifies available

CCMD intelligence capabilities and anticipated shortfalls, CSA and Service intelligence center estimates, the annex B (Intelligence) to a campaign or a contingency plan, and when appropriate a national intelligence support plan or the joint intelligence posture assessment.

Intelligence Support to Plan Assessment and Decision Making

Commanders continuously assess the OE and the progress of their campaigns, and then compare them to their initial vision and intent. The joint force J-2, through the CCMD JIOC, assesses adversary capabilities, vulnerabilities, and intentions and monitors the OE. The J-2 helps the commander and staff decide what aspects of the OE to measure and how to measure them to determine progress toward accomplishing a task, creating an effect, or achieving an objective. Intelligence personnel use the JIPOE process to provide JFCs and their staffs with a detailed understanding of the adversary and other relevant aspects of the OE.

Intelligence Support to Execution by Phase

Intelligence staffs must be familiar with specific phasing arrangements of each command OPLAN because the phasing may differ for specific types of operations. During execution, intelligence must stay at least one step ahead of operations and not only support the current phase of the operation, but also simultaneously lay the informational groundwork required for subsequent phases. Execution of joint operations requires optimizing the use of limited intelligence assets and maximizing the efficiency of intelligence production resources and is the ultimate test of the efficacy of intelligence support planning.

Joint, Interagency, and Multinational Intelligence Sharing and Cooperation

An Intelligence Sharing Environment

The success of joint and multinational operations and interorganizational coordination hinges upon timely and accurate information and intelligence sharing. To prevail, the JFC's decision and execution cycles must be consistently faster than the adversary's and be based on better information. Being faster and better requires having unfettered access to the tasking, collection, processing, analysis, and dissemination of information derived from all available sources. Cooperation, collaboration, and coordination are enabled by an intelligence and information environment that integrates joint, multinational, and interagency partners in a collaborative enterprise.

Principles for Multinational Intelligence Sharing

In most multinational operations, the JFC will be required to share intelligence with foreign military forces and to coordinate receiving intelligence from those forces. The principles for multinational intelligence sharing are: align with national disclosure policy; maintain unity of effort; make adjustments to resolve significant differences in intelligence doctrine and procedures; plan early and plan concurrently; share necessary information; and conduct complementary operations.

Principles for Interorganizational Intelligence Collaboration

Interagency intelligence collaboration should be encouraged whenever possible consistent with applicable national, agency, or organizational procedures and classification guidelines. The principles for interorganizational intelligence collaboration are: establish strong relationship networks; build mutual trust and respect for colleagues; share a common vision; minimize territorial issues; establish continuous communication; and eliminate impediments.

CONCLUSION

This publication is the keystone document for joint intelligence. It provides fundamental principles and guidance for intelligence support to joint operations.

CHAPTER I
THE NATURE OF INTELLIGENCE

"By 'intelligence' we mean every sort of information about the enemy and his country—the basis, in short, of our own plans and operations."

Carl von Clausewitz
***On War*, 1832**

1. Introduction

The management of and integration of intelligence into military operations are inherent responsibilities of command. These responsibilities are performed at every echelon of command and across the range of military operations. Technology enables joint force and component commanders and their staffs to access in near-real-time, very large amounts of information relating to aspects of the operational environment (OE)—the composite of the conditions, circumstances, and influences that affect the employment of capabilities and bear on the decisions of the commander. Information covering a wide range of issues relating to friendly, neutral, and adversary forces and the civilian populace will be available throughout the joint force. There will also be a large volume of information concerning weather, terrain, cultural influences, and other aspects of the OE. This mass of information can be distilled into intelligence to support a predictive estimate of the situation, as well as adversary capabilities and intentions. It is this estimative nature of intelligence that distinguishes it from the mass of other information available to the commander.

a. Information is of greatest value when it contributes to the commander's decision-making process by providing reasoned insight into future conditions or situations. This may occur as a result of its association with other information from the commander's experience. Raw data by itself has relatively limited utility. However, when data is collected from a sensor and processed into an intelligible form, it becomes information and gains greater utility. Information on its own may be of utility to the commander, but when related to other information about the OE and considered in the light of past experience, it gives rise to a new understanding of the information, which may be termed "intelligence." The foundation of the process that produces intelligence is built by analysts relating or comparing information against other information or a database, and drawing conclusions. The relationship between data, information, and intelligence is graphically depicted in Figure I-1. Ultimately, intelligence has two critical features that distinguish it from information. Intelligence allows anticipation or prediction of future situations and circumstances, and it informs decisions by illuminating the differences in available courses of action (COAs).

b. Intelligence provides the commander a variety of assessments and estimates that facilitate understanding the OE. Assessments are situational, for example some assessments will be threat-based providing an analysis of threat capabilities and intentions; others are population-based, providing the commander an analysis of sociocultural factors. With predictive, accurate, and relevant intelligence estimates, commanders gain an advantage in the OE by understanding an adversary's decision-making cycle, and possibly predicting and

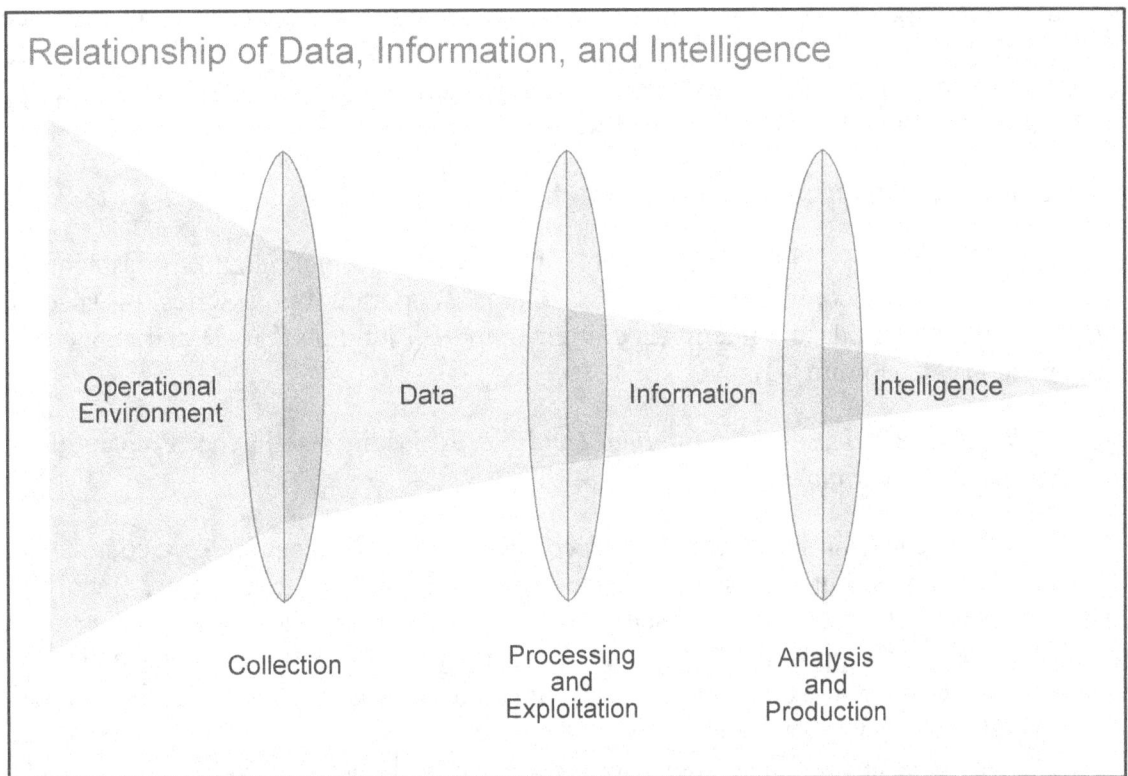

Figure I-1. Relationship of Data, Information, and Intelligence

countering adversarial operations. Regardless of the situation, intelligence assessments and estimates enable commanders to formulate plans and make better decisions based on this knowledge. Thus, predictive, accurate, and relevant intelligence can mitigate the risks inherent in military operations and increase the likelihood of success.

c. Intelligence is not an exact science; intelligence analysts will have some uncertainty as they assess the OE, as should the commander and staff as they plan and execute operations. Intelligence, as the synthesis of quantitative analysis and qualitative judgment is subject to competing interpretation. It is therefore important that intelligence analysts communicate the degree of confidence they have in their analytic conclusions. Such communication of analytic confidence helps intelligence consumers in deciding how much weight to place on intelligence assessments when making a decision. One methodology intelligence personnel may use to assign a confidence level to their analytic conclusions or intelligence assessments is discussed in Appendix A, "Intelligence Confidence Levels in Analytic Judgments."

d. Intelligence includes the organizations, capabilities, and processes involved in the collection, processing, exploitation, analysis, and dissemination of information or finished intelligence. Intelligence, however, is not an end in itself. To increase the operational relevance of intelligence, intelligence planners and managers should anticipate consumer needs. Thus, an examination of whether intelligence is effective or influential not only depends on the intelligence organizations, processes, and products, but must also examine users' intelligence needs. Explicit user requirements, identified and properly communicated to intelligence organizations by intelligence planners, initiate the appropriate intelligence activities. Intelligence products provide users with the information that has been collected and analyzed based on their requirements. It is important to remember that because the OE is dynamic, intelligence is a continuous activity.

2. The Roles and Responsibilities of Joint Intelligence

The primary role of joint intelligence is to provide information and assessments to facilitate mission accomplishment. This role is supported by a series of specific responsibilities to guide the intelligence directorate of a joint staff (J-2) and supporting organizations (see Figure I-2).

For further information, see Joint Publication (JP) 2-01.3, Joint Intelligence Preparation of the Operational Environment.

a. **Inform the Commander.** Intelligence directly supports the joint force commander (JFC) in planning, executing, and assessing the impact of those operations. The J-2 analyzes the adversary and other relevant aspects of the OE, and produces assessments on a continuing basis to support the commander in creating and/or exploiting opportunities to accomplish friendly force objectives. For example, to maintain the initiative, the JFC will seek to understand and potentially influence the adversary's decision-making process (e.g., the JFC will seek new and accurate intelligence that will enable friendly forces to take effective action faster than the adversary). The J-2 should assess the characteristics of the adversary's decision-making process and identify weaknesses that may be exploited. The J-2 should disseminate intelligence in a timely manner to the JFC, staff, and components.

b. **Describe the OE.** Present the OE as a confluence of the conditions, circumstances, and influences that affect the employment of friendly and adversary forces. Describing this OE to the commander and staff affects the commander's COA assessment, as well as future operations.

Responsibilities of Joint Intelligence

- Inform the commander.
- Describe the operational environment.
- Identify, define, and nominate objectives.
- Support the planning and execution of operations.
- Counter adversary deception and surprise.
- Support friendly deception efforts.
- Assess the effectiveness of operations.

Figure I-2. Responsibilities of Joint Intelligence

c. **Identify, Define, and Nominate Objectives.** All aspects of military planning are dependent on the determination of clearly defined, achievable, and measurable objectives. When identifying and nominating objectives, the J-2 should understand the command's responsibilities; the JFC's mission and intent; means available, including host nation and multinational forces, interagency partners, nongovernmental organizations (NGOs), and intergovernmental organizations (IGOs); the adversary; weather; and characteristics of the operational area. Intelligence should increase the commander's understanding of the threat and adversary's probable intentions, end states, objectives, most likely and most dangerous COAs, strengths, and critical capabilities. This allows the J-2 to recommend objectives, requirements, and centers of gravity (COGs). Once these objectives are approved by the commander, the J-2 must continuously review them with respect to the adversary and the changing situation to determine whether they remain relevant to the commander's intent.

d. **Support the Planning and Execution of Operations.** Commanders and staffs at all levels require intelligence to plan, direct, conduct, and assess operations. This intelligence is crucial to commanders, staffs, and components in identifying and selecting specific objectives and targets, associating them with desired effects, and determining the means to accomplish the JFC's overall mission. The J-2 supports the execution of the plan with the strategic, operational, and tactical intelligence needed to sustain the operation.

e. **Counter Adversary Deception and Surprise.** Joint force vulnerability to threat denial and deception will be determined, in large part, by the threat efforts to deny and deceive collection efforts. Intelligence analysts should remain sensitive to the possibility that they are being deceived and should consider all possible adversary capabilities and intentions. Similarly, analytical approaches that emphasize anomalies characterized by a lack of activity (e.g., absence of seasonal training, important persons missing from ceremonial events) are particularly valuable. To counter adversary deception efforts, intelligence analysts must confirm their analysis using multiple and proven analytical methods and processes (e.g., use of red teams, devil's advocates, alternative hypotheses).

f. **Support Friendly Deception Efforts.** Altering the perception of an adversary—to mislead or delude—helps achieve security and surprise. Intelligence and counterintelligence (CI) support effective friendly information operations (IO) through sociocultural analysis (SCA) of adversary leadership characteristics. The J-2 also assesses how the adversary is reacting to the friendly deception effort. Identifying deception objectives to complement operational objectives should be an interactive process, which is aided by the use of a red team or red cell.

For further information, see JP 3-13, Information Operations.

g. **Assess the Effectiveness of Operations.** Intelligence helps evaluate military operations by objectively assessing their impact on the adversary and other relevant aspects of the OE with respect to the JFC's intent and objectives. Intelligence should assist JFCs in determining if operations are producing desired or undesired effects, when objectives have been attained, and when unforeseen opportunities can be exploited or require a change in planned operations to respond to adversary (enemy) actions.

3. The Joint Intelligence Process

The joint intelligence process provides the basis for common intelligence terminology and procedures. It consists of six interrelated categories of intelligence operations characterized by broad activities conducted by intelligence staffs and organizations for the purpose of providing commanders and national-level decision makers with relevant and timely intelligence. The six categories of intelligence operations are: planning and direction; collection; processing and exploitation; analysis and production; dissemination and integration; and evaluation and feedback. In many situations, various intelligence operations occur almost simultaneously or may be bypassed. For example, a request for imagery requires planning and direction activities but may not involve new collection, processing, or exploitation. In this case, the imagery request could go directly to a production facility where previously collected and exploited imagery is reviewed to determine if it will satisfy the request. Likewise, during processing and exploitation, relevant information may be disseminated directly to the user without first undergoing detailed all-source analysis and intelligence production. Significant unanalyzed operational information and critical intelligence should be simultaneously available to both the commander (for time-sensitive decision-making) and to the all source intelligence analyst (for the production and dissemination of intelligence assessments and estimates). Additionally, the activities within each type of intelligence operation are conducted continuously and in conjunction with activities in each intelligence operation category. For example, intelligence planning (IP) occurs continuously while intelligence collection and production plans are updated as a result of previous requirements being satisfied and new requirements being identified. New requirements are typically identified through analysis and production and prioritized dynamically during the conduct of operations or through joint operation planning. The joint force's mission is determined during joint operation planning and provides the focal point around which the intelligence process is organized. A conceptual model of the intelligence process is depicted in Figure I-3.

The joint intelligence process is encompassed within the 2.0 series of tasks in Chairman of the Joint Chiefs of Staff Manual (CJCSM) 3500.04, Universal Joint Task Manual, which provides a common language and reference system to communicate mission requirements.

a. **Planning and Direction.** IP and direction is best understood as the development of intelligence plans and the continuous management of their execution. Planning and direction activities include, but are not limited to: the identification and prioritization of intelligence requirements; the development of concepts of intelligence operations and architectures required to support the commander's mission; tasking subordinate intelligence elements for the collection of information or the production of finished intelligence; submitting requests for additional capabilities to higher headquarters; and submitting requests for collection, exploitation, or all-source production support to external, supporting intelligence entities. IP and direction occurs continuously as the intelligence component of the command's campaign and contingency adaptive planning effort. IP for campaign plans allows for the prioritization of intelligence support across all ongoing operations and simultaneous planning efforts. On the other hand, IP for contingency plans informs the development of joint capabilities and enhances the readiness to respond to potential crises. The most likely threat scenarios are used as the core of the deliberate planning effort for potential contingency operations.

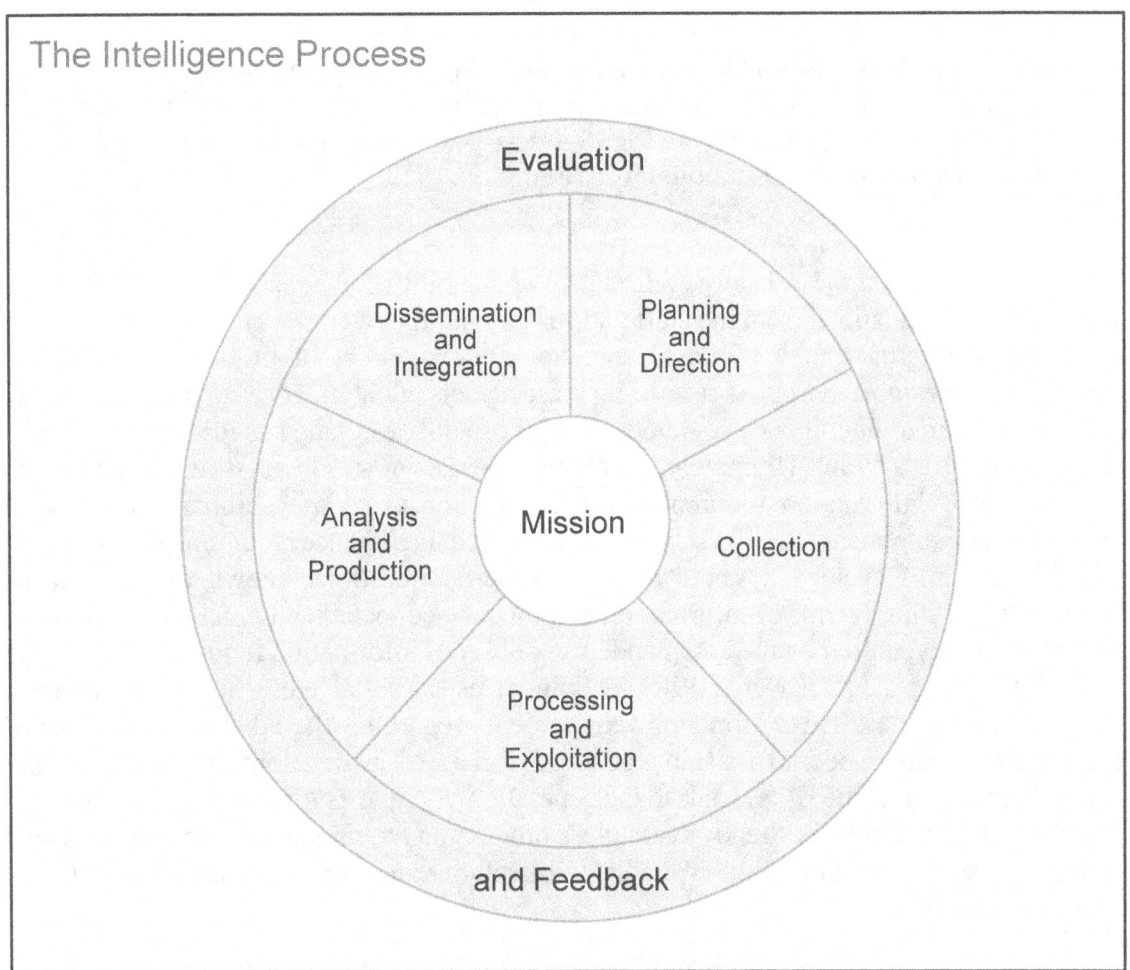

Figure I-3. The Intelligence Process

Through this effort, intelligence planners determine the personnel, equipment, and intelligence architecture essential for support to joint operations. When a particular crisis unfolds, commanders and their staffs develop an operation order (OPORD). Intelligence input to the OPORD includes an adjusted and updated threat scenario and an intelligence annex that tailors intelligence support to the nature and scope of operations to be conducted. Assessments conducted by intelligence personnel provide operation planners feedback for future planning for subsequent operations.

Intelligence support to joint operation planning is discussed in greater detail in Chapter IV, "Intelligence Support to Planning, Executing, and Assessing Joint Operations."

(1) **Intelligence Requirement and Information Requirement Planning.** During mission analysis, the joint force staff identifies significant information gaps about the adversary and other relevant aspects of the OE. After gap analysis, the staff formulates intelligence requirements, which are general or specific subjects upon which there is a need for the collection of information or the production of intelligence. All staff sections may recommend intelligence requirements for designation as priority intelligence requirements

KEY TERM:

Planning and Direction. In intelligence usage, the determination of intelligence requirements, development of appropriate intelligence architecture, preparation of a collection plan, issuance of orders and requests to information collection agencies.

(PIRs). However, the J-2 has overall staff responsibility for consolidating intelligence requirement nominations from the staff and for making the overall recommendation to the commander regarding their approval and their relative order of priority. Intelligence requirements designated as PIRs receive increased levels of intelligence support and priority in the allocation of intelligence resources while those not designated as PIR are satisfied as time and resources allow. Ultimately, the commander designates PIRs, which together with friendly force information requirements (FFIRs), constitute the commander's critical information requirements (CCIRs). Based on identified intelligence requirements (to include PIRs), the staff develops a series of more specific questions known as information requirements—those items of information that must be collected and processed to develop the intelligence required by the commander. A subset of information requirements that are related to and would answer a PIR are known as essential elements of information (EEIs)—the most critical information requirements regarding the adversary and the OE needed by the commander to assist in reaching a decision. The development of information requirements (to include EEIs) leads to the generation of requests for information (RFIs). If the required information is already available, a production requirement may be initiated, and if the required information is not available, a collection requirement is initiated. Figure I-4 illustrates this process.

(a) The JFC uses PIRs as a tool to designate intelligence that is critical to decision making, and to focus the intelligence system and the allocation of available intelligence capabilities. PIR nominations consider the mission, commander's intent, operational objectives, and the time frame of expected operations. The JFC develops PIRs that support critical decisions over the course of an operation, and for complex phased operations, develops separate PIRs for each phase. As an operation ensues, the commander updates PIRs to address new requirements or concerns, and as the situation changes, either eliminates some or develops others. A JFC's total number of PIRs for any phase of an operation should reflect a reasonable balance between mission critical requirements and finite intelligence support capability. Because of this, PIRs should be ranked and disseminated in priority of importance. Other valid intelligence requirements are submitted, but receive lower levels of intelligence support.

(b) Using PIRs as the basis, the intelligence staff develops the command's EEIs. To satisfy information requirements (to include EEIs), intelligence staffs should identify the specific indicators that could fill a gap in the command's knowledge and understanding of adversary activities and other relevant aspects of the OE.

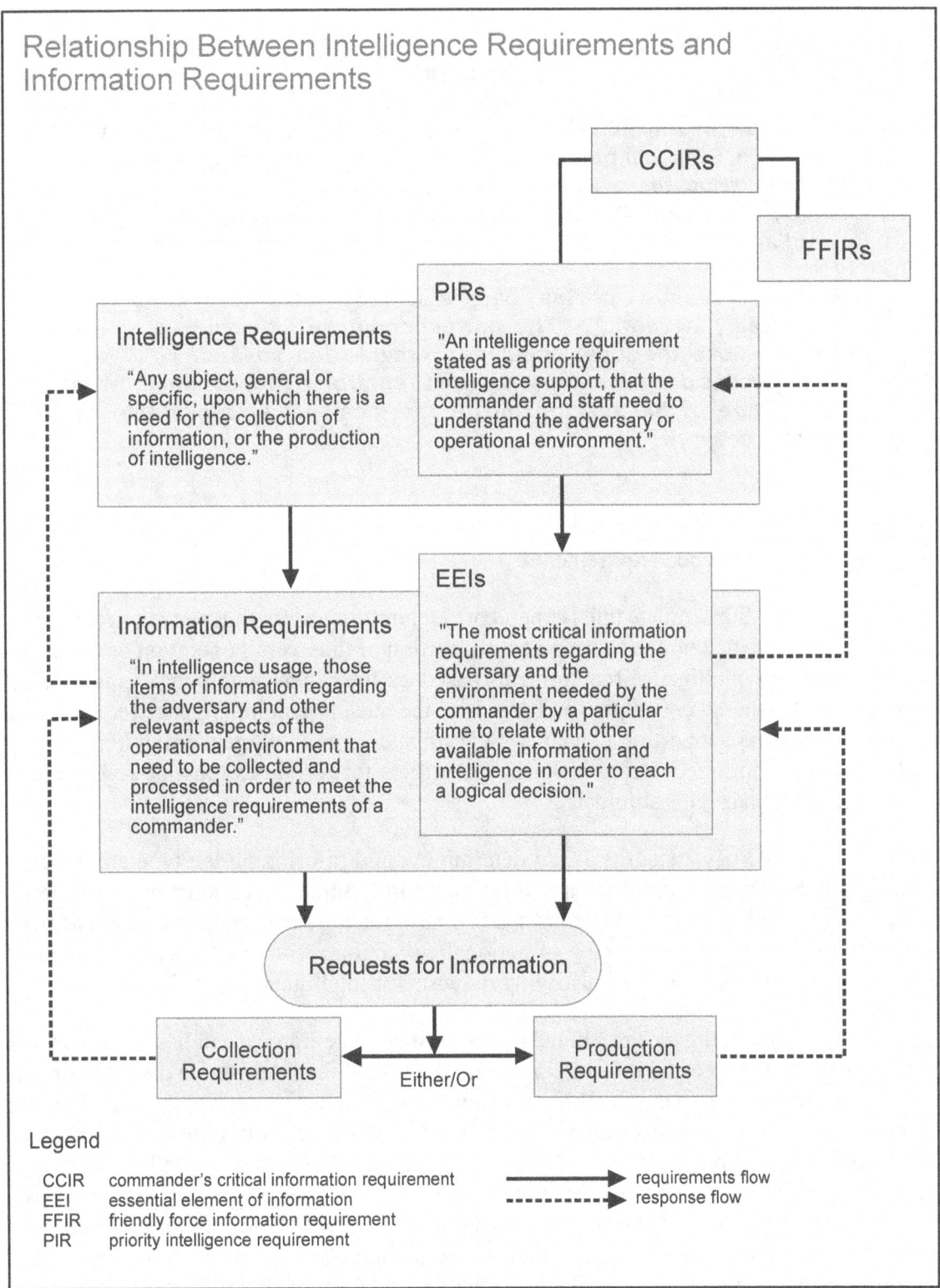

Figure I-4. Relationship Between Intelligence Requirements and Information Requirements

(c) In addition to joint forces intelligence requirements, the intelligence staff must be aware of the intelligence requirements of higher, adjacent, subordinate, and

PRIORITY INTELLIGENCE REQUIREMENT (PIR)/ESSENTIAL ELEMENT OF INFORMATION (EEI)

For example, if the PIR is "Will the enemy attack within the next 72 hours?", the EEIs will be questions such as "Where is the XX Armored Division?" "Has the artillery subordinate to the XX Corps deployed forward?" "Are aircraft being loaded with air-to-ground munitions at the forward airfields?" and "Where are the major surface combatants?"

A PIR for a non-state actor may be, "What is the level of local support for the adversary network?" The corresponding EEIs could be, "What resources does the local population provide the adversary?" "What coercive tactics does the adversary use to control the population?" "What is the nature of the relationship of the local power brokers to the adversary network?"

supported elements, the operational requirements of supported elements, as well as national-level intelligence requirements.

(d) Subordinate units expand on the joint forces intelligence requirements by making them specific enough to support their portion of the overall operation or campaign and also develop intelligence requirements based on their own operational requirements. The JFC's PIRs should encompass and prioritize the most urgent intelligence requirements of subordinate and supporting elements. Subordinate force intelligence requirements are addressed and prioritized during planning. Conflicts for resources must be resolved and unnecessary redundancies eliminated.

(e) PIRs assist the J-2 in determining and prioritizing the type and level of intelligence resources required to support the joint force. Intelligence staffs use intelligence requirements as a basis for: formulating statements of intelligence interest to the intelligence community (IC); justifying tasking of national collection resources through the Defense Intelligence Agency (DIA); and justifying requests for intelligence capabilities.

(f) Intelligence personnel review existing intelligence databases for potential solutions to intelligence and information requirements. If the intelligence does not already exist, the requestor issues an RFI—a specific time-sensitive ad hoc requirement for information or intelligence products, distinct from standing requirements or scheduled intelligence production. An RFI can be initiated at any level of command, and is validated in accordance with the combatant command's (CCMD's) procedures. An RFI leads to a production requirement, if the request can be answered with information on hand, or a collection requirement, if the request requires collection of new information. Anticipated production requirements are typically articulated in the form of analytic tasks and subtasks

KEY TERM:

Specific Information Requirement. A basic question that must be answered to satisfy a collection request.

during planning and entered into the appropriate RFI management system during execution. On the other hand, if an RFI leads to the initiation of a collection requirement, requestors of intelligence collection support should provide specific information requirements (SIRs) to allow the formulation of collection requirements and the allocation collection capabilities to satisfy them. If the requestor does not provide SIRs, the collection manager should consult with the requestor to determine the indicators of activity against which to focus collection capabilities so that appropriate SIRs can be developed.

(g) To the extent possible, identify PIRs, EEIs, associated analytic tasks, and SIRs in advance for each operational phase to provide the basis for synchronizing the reception and integration of required intelligence capabilities. Collection capability shortfalls identified during planning may form the basis for requests for forces (RFFs) and requests for support from national intelligence resources. This information ensures that the employment of defense intelligence capabilities is prioritized on supporting commanders in achieving their operational objectives.

(2) **Analysis and Production Planning.** All-source intelligence production is facilitated through a collaborative or federated effort in which information is rapidly shared among geographically dispersed organizations. This approach involves dividing the analysis and production effort among US and partner nation (PN) intelligence facilities and organizations worldwide to meet the intelligence needs of the joint force. Analysis and production responsibilities assigned during joint operation planning establish the anticipated flow of information and the development of the appropriate intelligence dissemination architecture.

(a) **Defense Intelligence Analysis Program (DIAP).** The DIAP establishes policy, procedures, and responsibilities for intelligence analysis and production within defense intelligence. The DIAP recognizes the overwhelming complexity of providing intelligence for worldwide operations, and therefore divides the analytic effort according to prioritized categories of defense topics, transnational issues, and countries.

(b) In many situations, the level of production, uniqueness of the product, or availability of personnel may require extensive lead time. For this reason, theater level and below intelligence planners should anticipate analytic tasks and identify the need to federate production with outside commands and agencies as early as possible. This includes production requirements that should be coordinated from tactical through national levels and access to intelligence and non-intelligence databases such as an automated biometric information system. Additionally, they should also work with the component intelligence elements to minimize confusion and duplication of effort by coordinating their respective roles and responsibilities with regard to analysis, production, and associated resources.

(3) **Collection and Exploitation Planning.** Collection planning matches anticipated collection requirements with appropriate theater and national collection capabilities. It is a continuous process that coordinates and integrates the efforts of all collection units and agencies. This multi-echelon collaboration helps identify collection gaps and redundant coverage in a timely manner to optimize the employment of all available collection capabilities.

(a) The IP component of the Adaptive Planning and Execution (APEX) system establishes collection planning procedures to be applied during joint operation planning. Conceptually, collection planning performed during joint operation planning precedes collection management performed during execution.

(b) **Intelligence, Surveillance, and Reconnaissance (ISR).** Collection operations are carried out during either surveillance or reconnaissance missions. While reconnaissance missions are specifically conducted to obtain information about the threat or the OE, surveillance missions consist of the systematic observation of places, persons, or things. To ensure these two types of missions are fully integrated into the overall joint operation, J-2 and operations directorate of a joint staff (J-3) staffs must continuously collaborate to synchronize the employment of assigned and allocable platforms and sensors against specified collection targets. They must also ensure raw data is routed to the appropriate processing and exploitation system so that it may be converted into useable information and disseminated to the user in a timely fashion. The J-2 is responsible for identifying potential collection targets and prioritizing anticipated collection requirements that are then used to drive surveillance and reconnaissance mission planning. The J-3 manages the operational area on behalf of the commander and deconflicts the physical employment of the various platforms with other operations to be conducted within the land, air, and maritime domains. Additionally, as the command's overall force manager, the J-3 recommends to the commander the apportionment of platforms to subordinate echelons so as to inform their planning efforts and in collaboration with the J-2 makes recommendations regarding their allocation during execution. Priorities for the apportionment and allocation of collection and exploitation capabilities to subordinate JFCs is typically based on the missions they've been assigned and the operational priorities set by the combatant commander (CCDR). Adaptive collection planning by the J-2 and continuous collaboration between the J-2 and J-3 staffs during reconnaissance and surveillance mission planning provides for the effective management and optimal employment of all available platforms, sensors, and associated processing, exploitation, and dissemination (PED) systems.

(c) Federated exploitation planning is typically conducted during joint operation planning based on anticipated single-source analytic throughput. It provides the appropriate intelligence systems architecture to route raw data to predetermined exploitation nodes or the end user.

(4) **Communications and Intelligence Systems Architecture Planning.** Intelligence dissemination requirements, systems, and procedures must be coordinated in advance with subordinate, adjacent, supporting, and higher intelligence organizations and commands, and with the communications system directorate of a joint staff (J-6). The management of information transmitted over communications paths is an important

---

KEY TERM:

Intelligence, Surveillance, and Reconnaissance. An activity that synchronizes and integrates the planning and operation of sensors, assets, and processing, exploitation, and dissemination systems in direct support of current and future operations. This is an integrated intelligence and operations function.

---

consideration to be made during joint operation planning. J-2 staffs must consider intelligence requirements when prioritizing information dissemination in terms of the product, foreign disclosure requirements, the available communications paths, and the time sensitivity of the product. Dissemination priorities must be updated throughout the course of the operation. Communications and intelligence systems architecture planning must ensure survivability, protection (or assurance), and interoperability of both information architectures and the information contained therein for all combinations of government and commercial configurations.

(5) **CI Planning.** CI focuses on the activities to protect against the harmful activities of outside entities. Coordination of CI activities must be accomplished during joint operation planning. Identification of ongoing and planned intelligence activities and JFC intentions will allow CI specialists to assess physical and personnel vulnerabilities and hostile forces capability to target military operations using technical means, terrorism, espionage, and sabotage, or to evoke a response such as a demonstration or strike. CI activities may also provide formal liaison with host nation, intelligence law enforcement, and security activities to support joint operations and to enhance the command's force protection efforts. The CI coordinating authority is appointed at the CCMD and joint task force (JTF) levels, and is responsible for synchronizing, coordinating, and deconflicting all CI activities within their respective operational areas.

(6) **Planning Intelligence Support to the Joint Targeting Cycle.** Target development and IP are interrelated. The intelligence staff of the JFC designated as a supported commander will lead the lethal and nonlethal target IP effort. During IP, the JFC should assess organic capabilities to support joint force selected COAs, determine related target intelligence shortfalls, and federate analytic tasks as required to support the joint targeting cycle. The intelligence staff develops supporting guidance in a targeting guidance message that delineates responsibilities for each phase of the joint targeting cycle. Based on the commander's objectives, and desired and undesired effects, targeteers begin a process of target system analysis (TSA) and target development. The target development process applies analysis and intelligence products developed through the joint intelligence preparation of the operational environment (JIPOE) process to evaluate relevant target systems and identify potential targets. As objects or entities are identified, they are vetted with the IC to verify their accuracy and characterization, validated by the commander to ensure they are valid and support military objectives, and added to the joint target list (JTL), the restricted target list (RTL), or no-strike list (NSL). If not validated, they are returned to the nominating organization for further development. The JTL contains targets which have military significance and do not have any employment restriction placed against them. The RTL contains targets which have military value, but because of operational considerations have specific restrictions placed on the actions authorized on them. Targets are approved by the JFC or directed by higher authorities. The NSL contains a list of objects or entities which are protected by the law of war, international law, or theater rules of engagement, national policy, or other restrictions, and, so long as they remain on the NSL, may not be struck. As targeteers develop these lists, they coordinate with all-source analysts and collection managers to gather additional information, imagery, and other intelligence products to provide a more complete picture of the enemy capabilities to fill intelligence gaps.

For further information on targeting, target development, target lists, and federated targeting, see JP 3-60, Joint Targeting, *JP 3-09,* Joint Fire Support, *Chairman of the Joint Chiefs of Staff Instruction (CJCSI) 3370.01,* Target Development Standards, *and CJCSM 3314.01A,* Intelligence Planning.

(7) **Other Planning**

(a) **Administration and Logistics Planning.** To ensure intelligence staffs are adequately filled, the J-2 should submit required joint intelligence manning document positions through the manpower and personnel directorate of the joint staff to ensure individual augmentee slots are filled with qualified personnel. Likewise, logistic requirements should be identified as early as possible to the joint forces logistics directorate, lift and transportation requirements in the time-phased force and deployment data to the J-3, and communications requirements for intelligence operations to the J-6. Additional functions that should be addressed as part of the planning and direction effort include: financial, contracting, training, and personnel support; physical and personnel security matters; intelligence and CI oversight compliance; inspector general issues; releasability and disclosure policy; and Freedom of Information Act guidance.

Additional guidance on augmentation is provided in JP 1-0, Joint Personnel Support.

(b) **Future Joint Intelligence Architecture Planning.** Shortfalls identified during the IP process may help determine intelligence organizational changes, personnel, and equipment requirements, and establish requirements for future capabilities and associated joint intelligence architectures.

(8) **Collection Management.** If during the conduct of operations, it is determined that an RFI must be converted into a collection requirement, a nomination for collection is submitted and collection management begins. Collection management is the process of converting intelligence-related information requirements into collection requirements, establishing priorities, tasking or coordinating with appropriate collection sources or agencies, monitoring results, and retasking, as required. Anchored on the appropriate collection management authority (CMA), collection management is composed of two components, collection requirements management (CRM) and collection operations management (COM).

(a) CRM is the authoritative development and control of collection, processing, exploitation, and information reporting requirements. This process normally results with the collection manager either tasking requirements to units over which the commander has authority, or generating requests to CMAs at a higher, lower, or lateral echelons to accomplish the collection mission. During CRM all collection requirements are prioritized and appropriately registered. Prioritization should be based on the commander's intent, objectives, approved PIRs, and the current situation to ensure that limited assets or resources are directed against the most critical requirements. A coordinated, coherent, target-specific strategy is developed to satisfy validated and prioritized collection requirements. The collection strategy is a scheme for collecting information from all available sources to satisfy SIRs. The scheme is applied as discipline-specific collection requirements are sent to internal intelligence organizations for tasking, or are submitted for validation and tasking requests to external organizations or agencies. Activities then transition from CRM to COM.

(b) COM is the authoritative direction, scheduling, and control of specific collection operations and associated processing, exploitation, and information reporting resources. This includes the selection and tasking of specific assets and sensors. The collection operations manager synchronizes the timing of collection with the operational scheme of maneuver and with other intelligence operations such as processing and exploitation, analysis and production, and dissemination. The collection operations manager then selects assets best suited to collect the information needed to satisfy the SIR. The collection operations manager prepares or revises the command's intelligence collection plan to efficiently and effectively meet collection requirements and tasks collection assets with sufficient direction to accomplish the mission. The collection operations manager develops and coordinates sensor employment guidance that helps to refine collection plans and strategies and enables the optimum employment of collection capabilities to collection requirements.

(c) Collection managers must know of the capabilities, limitations, survivability, and lead times of available collection systems, as well as the processing and exploitation, analysis, and production timelines to complete and disseminate a product. Collection managers must be able to coordinate the employment of all available collection capabilities. This includes requesting external theater and national level resources to acquire needed information.

(d) To minimize the effects of enemy deception, and provide the JFC the most accurate intelligence possible, analysis of information from a variety of collection sources is required so information from one source can be verified or confirmed by others. Multiple collection sources enable collection managers to cross-cue between different sources (e.g., using signals intelligence [SIGINT] direction finding to focus collection by geospatial intelligence [GEOINT] systems). A challenge inherent to using a multidiscipline collection is the need to avoid an ad hoc approach and to establish procedures beforehand that support tipping, hand-off, cross-cueing, or retasking of one asset in support of another. Collection systems also need redundancy so that the loss or failure of one collection capability can be compensated for by alternate capabilities. However, careful consideration must be given to having multiple collection sources performing redundant collection, as collection requirements will usually exceed collection, processing, and exploitation capacity. This supports the collection management principle of using a multidiscipline approach.

(e) To effectively integrate intelligence support to operations, the intelligence staff and the operations staff must work closely together. Collection managers, targeteers, and intelligence analysts collaborate to anticipate collection requirements, validate preplanned collection tasks, and update adaptive collection plans. The joint force may establish a joint collection management board (JCMB) to monitor and update collection requirements and asset status, and recommends the revised collection plan for approval by the commander. Active involvement of targeteers, analysts, and J-3 personnel in concert with the collection managers is critical to the success of the JCMB. Collection managers in coordination with (ICW) CCMD intelligence planners must ensure that the collection plan is synchronized with the operation plan (OPLAN) so that collection efforts are focused correctly at critical times. Additionally, reconnaissance and surveillance operations should be integrated with other forms of intelligence collection operations and coordinated with CI activities.

(f) There are numerous legal considerations associated with intelligence collection on US persons. Commanders and their intelligence staffs must be fully cognizant of their intelligence oversight responsibilities as delineated in Department of Defense (DOD) 5240.1-R, *Procedures Governing the Activities of DOD Intelligence Components That Affect United States Persons.* Prior to conducting collection on US persons, the Secretary of Defense (SecDef) will designate specific ISR platforms and associated PED capabilities to support incident awareness and assessment (IAA) requirements. Intelligence collection activities should be coordinated with the servicing staff judge advocate to ensure compliance with the law and any existing rules of engagement.

See JP 2-01, Joint and National Intelligence Support to Military Operations, *for more discussion on intelligence requirements and collection.*

b. **Collection.** Collection includes those activities related to the acquisition of data required to satisfy the requirements specified in the collection strategy. This is managed by collection managers, whose duties include selecting the most appropriate, available asset(s) and associated PED and then tasking selected asset(s) and associated PED to conduct collection missions. Collection managers also develop and coordinate sensor employment guidance, exercise authoritative control of specific collection operations, revise collection activities as required, monitor the overall satisfaction of requirements, and assess the effectiveness of the collection plan to satisfy the original and evolving intelligence needs. When opportunities arise, collection managers may direct dynamic cross-cueing of sensors to obtain a multidiscipline approach and obtain higher confidence data. When adjustments to the collection plan (or dynamic retasking of assets) are made, collection managers will inform other relevant stakeholders of the changes. Collectors, whether conducting reconnaissance and surveillance via technical means or human ones, obtain the data needed to satisfy the information requirements within the collection requirements tasked to them. Collected data is distributed via appropriately classified media/circuits to processing and exploitation elements. Collection managers continuously monitor the results not only of intelligence collection, but also processing and exploitation, and information reporting to determine if SIRs are being satisfied. Collection managers continuously assess the effectiveness of the collection plan in meeting the JFC's requirements as part of the command's evaluation and feedback portion of the intelligence process.

c. **Processing and Exploitation.** During processing and exploitation, raw collected data is converted into forms that can be readily used by commanders, decision makers at all levels, intelligence analysts and other consumers. Processing and exploitation includes first phase imagery exploitation, data conversion and correlation, document and media translation, and signal decryption, as well as reporting the results of these actions to analysis and production elements. Processing and exploitation may be federated or performed by the same element that collected the data. Federated exploitation planning is typically conducted during joint operation planning based on anticipated single-source analytic throughput and it ensures appropriate intelligence systems architecture is in place to route raw data to predetermined exploitation nodes.

(1) An example of processing and exploitation occurs when the technical parameters (frequency, pulse repetition frequency, and bandwidth) detected by an electronic intelligence (ELINT) collection system are compared and associated with the known parameters of a particular radar system. Rather than providing an analyst with an overwhelming mass of raw ELINT data, the analyst is provided with the essential fact.

(2) Different types of data require different degrees of processing before they can be intelligible to the recipient. In the area of SIGINT, processing and exploitation are increasingly automated and are being quickly performed by the collection systems. Similarly, captured enemy documents may only require translating before they can be used by analysts. On the other hand, the technical exploitation of an item of enemy equipment may require months of intensive effort before its full capabilities can be determined.

d. **Analysis and Production.** During analysis and production, intelligence is produced from the information gathered by the collection capabilities assigned or attached to the joint force and from the refinement and compilation of intelligence received from subordinate units and external organizations. All available processed information is integrated, evaluated, analyzed, and interpreted to create products that will satisfy the commander's PIRs or RFIs. Intelligence products can be presented in many forms. They may be oral presentations, hard copy publications, or electronic media. Intelligence production for joint operations is accomplished by units and organizations at every echelon. Federated production plans developed through IP are intended to provide reachback support to meet the CCDR's intelligence requirements. Whereas collection, processing, and exploitation are primarily performed by specialists from one of the major intelligence disciplines, analysis and production is done primarily by all-source analysts that fuse together information from all intelligence disciplines. The product of multidiscipline fusion effort is all-source intelligence. All source intelligence should comply with *Intelligence Community Directive #203*, Analytic Standards.

(1) A key methodology or process for conducting intelligence analysis and production is the **JIPOE** process.

(a) **JIPOE** is the continuous process through which J-2 manages the analysis and development of products that help the commander and staff understand the complex and interconnected OE—the composite of the conditions, circumstances, and influences that affect the employment of capabilities that bear on the decisions of the commander. The J-2 manages the JIPOE process with input from intelligence planners and other staff directorates or elements, such as medical and engineering, see Figure I-5.

(b) Analysts use the JIPOE process to analyze, correlate, and fuse information pertaining to all relevant aspects of the OE (e.g., political, military, economic, social, information, and infrastructure [PMESII] systems). The process is also used to analyze adversary capabilities, identify potential adversary COAs, and assess the most likely and

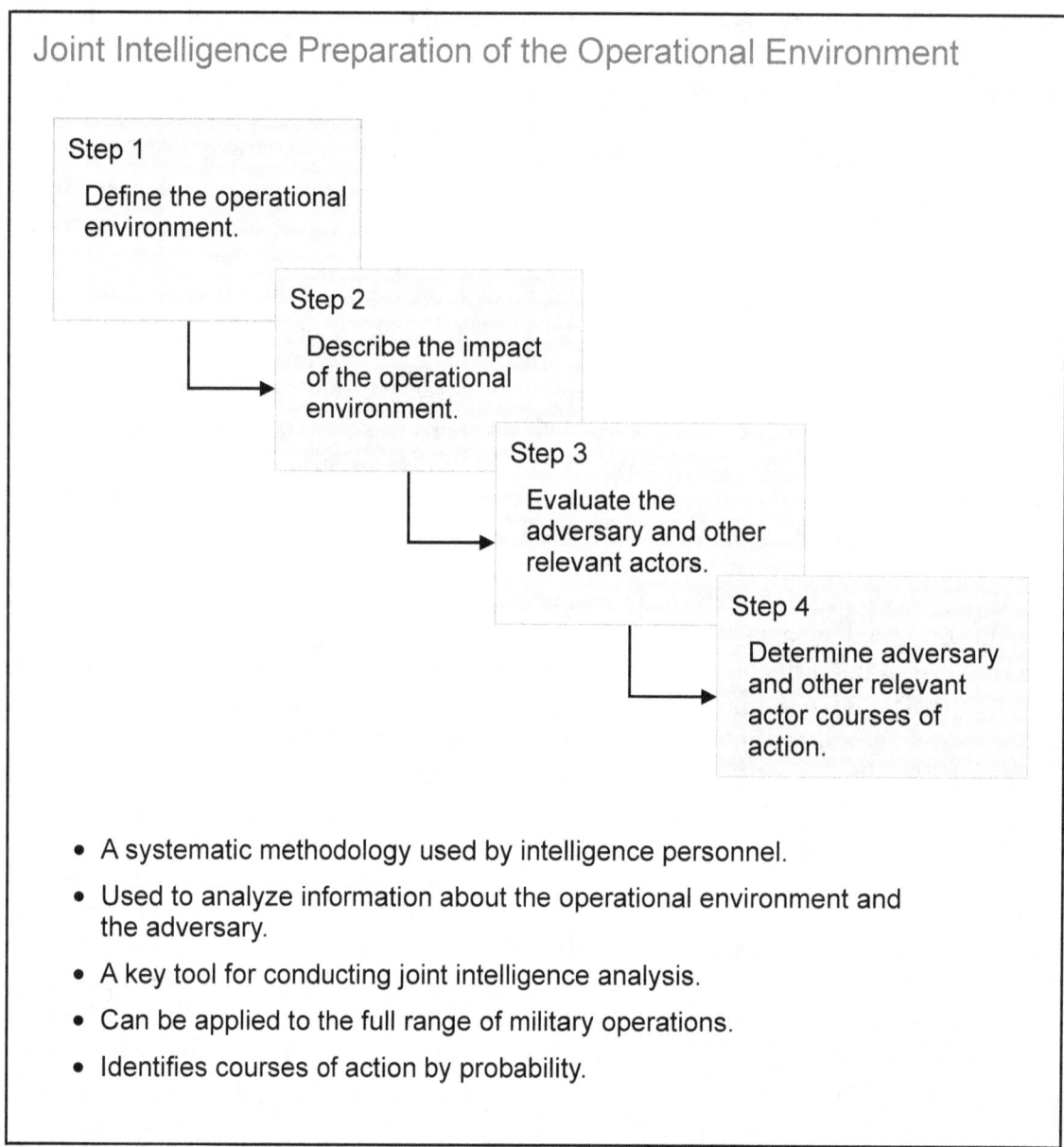

Figure I-5. Joint Intelligence Preparation of the Operational Environment

most dangerous adversary COAs. The process can be applied to the full range of military operations and to each level of war.

(c) Throughout the JIPOE process, at every echelon and production category, one of the most important, but least understood, aspects of analysis is SCA. SCA is the study, evaluation, and interpretation of information about adversaries and relevant actors through the lens of group-level decision making to discern catalysts of behavior and the context that shapes behavior. SCA informs the commander's understanding of adversaries and other relevant actors by analyzing societies, populations, and other groups of people, including their activities, relationships, and perspectives across time and space at varying scales of analysis. SCA includes the graphic representation of social and cultural information for a given area presented spatially (on a map) and temporally. SCA also includes the systematic mapping of human factors affecting a leader's or key actor's decision-making influences. SCA considers: relationships and activities of the population; social network analysis (looking at the interpersonal, professional, and social networks tied to an individual); as well as small and large group dynamics.

The JIPOE process is described in detail in JP 2-01.3, Joint Intelligence Preparation of the Operational Environment.

(2) Intelligence products are generally placed in one of eight production categories: warning, current, general military, target, scientific and technical (S&T), CI, identity intelligence (I2), and estimative intelligence (see Figure I-6). The categories are distinguished from each other primarily by the purpose for which the intelligence was produced. The categories can and do overlap, and the same intelligence and information can be used in each of the categories.

(a) **Warning Intelligence.** Warning provides a distinct communication to a decision maker about threats against US security, interests, or citizens. Warning carries a sense of urgency, implying the decision maker should take action to deter or mitigate the threat's impact. Warning analysis focuses on the opportunities to counter and alter only those threats that have detrimental effects for the US. This includes US military or political decision cycles, infrastructure, COA, or loss of governance. Defense intelligence recognizes two types of warning: emerging and enduring. "Emerging warning concerns" and "enduring warning problems" discuss issues relevant to national security warranting DOD leadership attention. Emerging warning issues may be ambiguous, and may be formalized as an "enduring warning problem" based on a risk evaluation to national security and planning guidance. The latter is usually linked to contingency plans, which are defined and longstanding potential threats to US interests.

(b) **Current Intelligence.** Current intelligence provides updated support for ongoing operation. It involves the integration of time-sensitive, all-source intelligence and

---

Categories of Intelligence Products

- Warning intelligence
- Current intelligence
- General military intelligence
- Target intelligence
- Scientific and technical intelligence
- Counterintelligence
- Estimative intelligence
- Identity intelligence

Figure I-6. Categories of Intelligence Products

---

information into concise, objective reporting on the current situation in a particular area. The term "current" is relative to the time sensitivities of the decision maker and the context of the type of operation being supported. For example, in some contexts intelligence may be considered "current," whereas other circumstances may require intelligence in near real time.

(c) **General Military Intelligence (GMI).** GMI focuses on the military capabilities of foreign countries and organizations, to include non-state actors, and other topics that could affect potential US or multinational military operations. This broad category of intelligence is normally associated with long-term planning, and attempts to identify and monitor trends affecting national security to facilitate the efficient application of finite resources. GMI is tailored to specific subordinate joint force missions and includes information on the organization, operations, facilities, and capabilities of selected foreign military forces. GMI also includes other relevant characteristics of the OE.

See JP 2-01, Joint and National Intelligence Support to Military Operations, *for more detailed discussion of GMI. See JP 4-02,* Health Service Support, *for more information on medical intelligence (MEDINT).*

(d) **Target Intelligence.** Target intelligence portrays and locates the components of a target or target complex, networks, and support infrastructure, and indicates its vulnerability and relative importance to the adversary. Target intelligence includes the characterization of a target and indicates its vulnerability, placement in larger systems or networks, and relative importance to the adversary. Characterization includes analyses of physical and virtual attributes (including the biographic, biologic, behavioral, and reputational attributes of human targets, to support weaponeering) and signatures (to support target detection and positive identification). Target intelligence also includes battle damage assessment (BDA) composed of physical damage/change assessment, functional damage/change assessment, and functional assessment of the higher level target system resulting from the application of lethal or nonlethal military force. It is critical that intelligence analysis supporting targeting remain consistent throughout the joint force. Target intelligence must holistically analyze the target so it can support all target engagement options. Throughout the targeting process, intelligence personnel should ensure that available information is considered to support proper target nomination, target development, and assessment. Target intelligence includes nominations for the NSL and RTL.

See JP 3-60, Joint Targeting, *and CJCSI 3370.01,* Target Development Standards, *for further information.*

(e) **Scientific and Technical Intelligence (S&TI).** S&TI examines foreign developments in basic and applied sciences and technologies with warfare potential, particularly enhancements to weapon systems. It includes S&TI characteristics, capabilities, vulnerabilities, and limitations of weapon systems, subsystems, and associated material, as well as related research and development. S&TI also addresses overall weapon systems, tactics analysis, and equipment effectiveness.

(f) **CI.** CI is information gathered and activities conducted to identify, deceive, exploit, disrupt, or protect against espionage, other intelligence activities, sabotage, or assassinations conducted for or on behalf of foreign powers, organizations, or persons, or their agents, or international terrorist organizations or activities. CI includes conducting strategic CI analysis to identify and produce finished intelligence on the foreign intelligence entities threat to DOD. CI develops and implements strategies and action plans to counter the CI threat, tasks CI collection capabilities, and leverages human intelligence (HUMINT), SIGINT, GEOINT, measurement and signature intelligence (MASINT), and open-source intelligence (OSINT) to fill CI collection gaps.

(g) **Estimative Intelligence.** Estimates are forecasts of current or potential situations with implications for planning and executing military operations. Estimative intelligence includes a description of relevant actors' capabilities, and reporting of their activities, and it analyzes known factors using techniques such as pattern analysis, inference, and statistical probability to address unresolved variables. A key to this predictive art is to provide commanders and planners with an assessment of relevant actors' responses based on friendly force actions.

(h) **I2.** I2 results from the fusion of identity attributes (biologic, biographic, behavioral, and reputational information related to individuals) and other information and intelligence associated with those attributes collected across all intelligence disciplines. I2 utilizes enabling intelligence activities, like biometrics-enabled intelligence (BEI), forensics-enabled intelligence (FEI), and document and media exploitation (DOMEX), to discover the existence of unknown potential threat actors by connecting individuals to other persons, places, events, or materials, analyzing patterns of life, and characterizing their level of potential threats to US interests.

e. **Dissemination and Integration.** During dissemination and integration, intelligence is delivered to and used by the consumer. Dissemination is facilitated by a variety of means. The means are determined by the needs of the user and the implications and criticality of the intelligence. Personal, networked, and database data transfers are all means of dissemination. The diversity of dissemination paths reinforces the need for communications and computer systems interoperability among joint and multinational forces, component commands, DOD organizations, and the interagency community.

(1) The Global Command and Control System and the DOD Distributed Common Ground/Surface Systems portray an integrated common operational picture (COP), built on a foundation of geospatial information, that displays the disposition of friendly, neutral, and adversary forces throughout the OE. Command and control, initiative, flexibility, and decision making are enhanced by an accurate and timely COP.

(2) The globally integrated architecture for intelligence dissemination should facilitate the timely communication of collected data, processed information, and fused intelligence among dispersed producers and consumers. The dissemination architecture allows intelligence organizations external to the joint force to address joint force intelligence needs through preplanned PIRs. Additionally, intelligence organizations should push intelligence to the consumer (using the most expeditious means available), and accommodate the consumer's pull on demand (allowing automated access to theater and national databases). This construct delivers timely intelligence and ISR-derived information, makes

maximum use of automation, and minimizes the flow of RFI messages and intelligence reports. The integrated broadcast service and the tactical related applications are examples of over-the-air updates that provide time-sensitive intelligence to tactical commanders.

Chapter V, "Joint, Interagency, and Multinational Intelligence Sharing and Cooperation," provides a more comprehensive discussion of intelligence dissemination architectures and requirements.

(3) Supporting intelligence organizations should provide intelligence to the consumer using the best available, and most secure, technology. Intelligence organizations at all levels should use precise terminology to minimize the possibility of confusion on the part of users reviewing assessments and estimates.

(4) Intelligence organizations should initiate and maintain close contact with users, ensure users are receiving their products promptly, and confirm those products fulfill requirements. The follow-up is a key part of the feedback process detailed in Figure I-3.

(5) After intelligence products are delivered, intelligence personnel and organizations are responsible for continuing to support users as they integrate the intelligence into their decision-making and planning processes. Products may require further clarification or they may raise new issues that need to be addressed. Additionally, products may need to be related to a larger intelligence picture, or may require reinterpretation due to changes in the OE.

(6) Rather than being the end of a process, the integration of intelligence is a continuous dialogue between the user and the producer. How intelligence is used is ultimately up to the user. The role of the producer is to provide the user with the best intelligence possible.

f. **Evaluation and Feedback.** Evaluation and feedback occur continuously throughout the intelligence process and as an assessment of the intelligence process as a whole. Intelligence personnel at all levels should assess the execution of the intelligence tasks they perform and gauge their impacts. Evaluation and feedback requires a collaborative dialogue between intelligence planners, collection managers, collectors, single and all-source analysts, and intelligence systems architects to identify deficiencies within the intelligence process. It also requires consultation with intelligence consumers to determine if intelligence requirements are being satisfied. Immediate applications of evaluation and feedback may include, but are not limited to, the rephrasing of an intelligence requirement for clarity, the dynamic retasking of a sensor, the rerouting of data to an alternate exploitation node, or the revision of an information report or a finished intelligence product. The goal of evaluation and feedback is to identify issues as early as possible to minimize information gaps and to mitigate capability shortfalls.

(1) Information gathered during evaluation and feedback may inform broader assessments of the intelligence staff function. Assessments provide leaders with the information to make decisions about reprioritization of intelligence requirements, shifts in

collection emphasis, changes to analytic levels of effort, reallocation of available intelligence assets, training of intelligence personnel, and the development of new intelligence capabilities.

(2) To perform assessments of the intelligence staff function, intelligence personnel develop intelligence measures of performance (MOPs) and intelligence measures of effectiveness (MOEs). These measures are informed by a variety of indicators related to the conduct of intelligence tasks or their impact. Task-related metrics are informed by indicators that are quantitative in nature. They determine whether a particular platform or sensor is performing according to technical specifications, the number of sorties conducted, the number of images taken, or the number of interrogations conducted or all-source products generated. On the other hand, effectiveness of intelligence operations is determined by gauging the impact of intelligence tasks performed within the intelligence process. Effectiveness-related metrics are informed by indicators that tend to be qualitative in nature. Factors considered in determining the effectiveness of intelligence operations include the reliability of a source, whether a particular information reported is considered actionable, or if a particular product is cited in finished intelligence as contributing to an increase in analytic confidence. Establishing MOEs requires addressing the question of intelligence or information value. The value of information or intelligence is tied to the decision which it supports and the amount of uncertainty it clarifies or resolves. Ultimately, the effectiveness of intelligence operations is assessed by devising metrics and indicators associated with the attributes of intelligence excellence discussed in Chapter II, "Principles of Joint Intelligence." The ability of the intelligence staff to assess the totality of intelligence operations relies on product satisfaction as determined by the user. For this reason, a feedback mechanism from the user should be consistent and of a formal nature with some element of systematic analysis to offer some rigor to the process.

(3) The establishment of formal assessment methods and procedures for the intelligence staff provides decision makers with actionable data backed by analytical rigor. Assessors must collect, evaluate, and understand the significance of data regarding both the conduct of intelligence tasks (intelligence MOPs) and the effectiveness of intelligence (intelligence MOEs) in satisfying the requirements of the commander and staff. Data resulting from assessments will support the identification and resolution of procedural issues and contribute to advocacy in resolving gaps and shortfalls.

(4) Sharing. Identify issues and lessons learned and report them. CJCSI 3150.25, *Joint Lessons Learned Program (JLLP)*, provides basic guidance and direction on establishing internal lessons learned programs and how to enter issues into a resolution process.

(5) Advocating Resolution. The goal of the evaluation and feedback step is that issues are identified and addressed within the joint intelligence process. Following the procedures of the JLLP facilitates issue tracking until resolved.

(6) CCMDs, Services, and combat support agencies (CSAs) are responsible to provide specific guidance to enable collection and distribution of observations of joint operations with assigned forces or personnel. It is essential that intelligence organizations

outside the joint force fully participate in the JLLP process to ensure that the benefits of lessons learned are disseminated as widely as possible.

4. Intelligence and the Levels of War

a. **Levels of War.** JP 3-0, *Joint Operations,* discusses three levels of war: strategic, operational, and tactical. Figure I-7 shows how intelligence operations support each level of war. The levels clarify links between strategic objectives, effects, and tactical actions and enable commanders to visualize a logical flow of operations, resource allocation, and tasks. Often, the accuracy of strategic, operational, or tactical labels can only be determined during post-mission analysis or historical studies.

(1) All levels of war have corresponding levels of intelligence operations. The construct of strategic, operational, and tactical levels of intelligence helps commanders and their J-2s visualize the flow of intelligence from one level to another. This construct facilitates the allocation of required collection, analytical, and dissemination resources and permits the assignment of appropriate intelligence tasks to national, theater, component, and supporting intelligence elements.

(2) Intelligence operations support commanders at all levels, both horizontally and vertically. Strategic intelligence operations provide continuity and depth of coverage even while the joint force is deploying. During campaign planning, strategic and operational intelligence operations focus on providing to the JFC information required to identify the adversary's COGs, COAs, vulnerabilities, and high-value targets (HVTs). During execution, operational intelligence operations provide the JFC with relevant, timely, and accurate intelligence relating to the accomplishment of campaign or major operation objectives.

(3) Levels of command, size of units, types of equipment, or types of forces or components are not associated with a particular level of intelligence operations. National assets such as intelligence and communications satellites, usually considered in a strategic context, are an important enabler of tactical operations. Conversely, troops operating in the field can gather intelligence of strategic importance.

(4) Operational and tactical intelligence operations provide the JFC the information required to identify adversary critical vulnerabilities, COGs, and critical nodes for the optimum application of all available resources, thereby allowing the JFC to most effectively employ the joint force. Figure I-7 depicts the levels of intelligence.

b. **Strategic Intelligence**

(1) **National strategic intelligence** is produced for the President, the National Security Council, Congress, SecDef, senior military leaders, CCDRs, and other US Government departments and agencies. It is used to develop national strategy and policy, monitor the international and global situation, prepare military plans, determine major weapon systems and force structure requirements, and conduct strategic operations. Strategic intelligence operations also produce the intelligence required by CCDRs to prepare strategic estimates, strategies, and plans to accomplish missions assigned by higher authorities. In addition to this focus primarily on the military instrument of national power,

```
┌─────────────────────────────────────────────────────────────────────┐
│                                                                       │
│  Levels of Intelligence                                               │
│                                                                       │
│   Strategic                                                           │
│     Senior Military and Civilian Leaders                              │
│     Combatant Commanders                                              │
│                                                                       │
│       • Assist in developing national strategy and policy.            │
│       • Monitor the international or global situation.                 │
│       • Assist in developing military plans.                          │
│       • Assist in determining major weapon systems and force          │
│         structure requirements.                                       │
│       • Support the conduct of strategic operations.                  │
│                                                                       │
│   Operational                                                         │
│     Combatant and Subordinate Joint Force Commanders                  │
│     and Component Commanders                                          │
│                                                                       │
│       • Focus on military capabilities and intentions of enemies      │
│         and adversaries.                                              │
│       • Analyze the operational environment.                          │
│       • Identify adversary centers of gravity and critical            │
│         vulnerabilities.                                              │
│       • Monitor events in the joint force commander's area of         │
│         interest.                                                     │
│       • Support the planning and conduct of joint campaigns.          │
│                                                                       │
│   Tactical                                                            │
│     Commanders                                                        │
│                                                                       │
│       • Support planning and the execution of battles, engagements,   │
│         and other joint force activities.                             │
│       • Provide commanders with information on imminent threats to    │
│         their forces and changes in the operational environment.      │
│       • Provide commanders with obstacle intelligence.                │
│                                                                       │
└─────────────────────────────────────────────────────────────────────┘
```

Figure I-7. Levels of Intelligence

strategic intelligence also allows for national leadership to determine potential options using the nonmilitary instruments of national power (diplomatic, informational, and economic) based on estimated opposing force or adversary reaction to US actions.

(2) **Theater strategic intelligence** supports joint operations across the range of military operations, assesses the current situation, and estimates future capabilities and intentions of adversaries that could affect the national security and US or allied interests. Theater strategic intelligence includes determining when, where, and in what strength the adversary will stage and conduct theater level campaigns and strategic unified operations.

c. **Operational Intelligence**

(1) Operational intelligence is primarily used by CCDRs and subordinate JFCs and their component commanders. Operational intelligence focuses on answering the commander's PIRs, assessing the effectiveness of operations, maintaining situational awareness of adversary military disposition, capabilities, and intentions, and other relevant aspects of the OE. Operational intelligence helps commanders keep abreast of events within

their area of interest (AOI) and helps them determine when, where, and in what strength the adversary might stage and conduct campaigns and major operations.

(2) Operational intelligence also includes monitoring terrorist incidents and natural or man-made disasters and catastrophes. During counterinsurgency and counterterrorism operations, operational intelligence is increasingly concerned with stability operations and has a greater focus on PMESII factors. It also assists commanders in assessing and evaluating actions and possible implications associated with noncombat operations such as foreign humanitarian assistance.

d. **Tactical Intelligence**

(1) Tactical intelligence is used by commanders, planners, and operators for planning and conducting battles, engagements, and special missions. Relevant, accurate, and timely tactical intelligence allows tactical units to achieve positional and informational advantage over their adversaries. Precise threat location, tracking, and target capabilities and status, in particular, are essential for success during actual mission execution. In addition, a key element of tactical intelligence is post-strike combat assessment, which is used by commanders and planners to determine the need to dynamically retask assets to restrike identified targets.

(2) Tactical intelligence addresses the threat across the range of military operations. Tactical intelligence operations identify and assess the adversary's capabilities, intentions, and vulnerabilities, as well as describe the physical environment. Tactical intelligence seeks to identify when, where, and in what strength the adversary will conduct tactical level operations. During counterinsurgency and counterterrorism operations, tactical intelligence is increasingly focused on identifying threats to stability operations. Together with CI, tactical intelligence will provide the commander with information on the imminent threats to the force from terrorists, saboteurs, insurgents and their networks, and foreign intelligence collection. The physical identification of the adversary and their operational networks allow for enhanced situational awareness, targeting, and watchlisting to track, hinder, or prevent insurgent movements within the region, nation, or international levels.

5. **Intelligence and the Range of Military Operations**

JP 3-0, *Joint Operations,* divides the range of military operations into three major types: military engagement, security cooperation, and deterrence; crisis response and limited contingency operations; and major operations and campaigns. While intelligence operations continue throughout the range of military operations, peacetime intelligence operations provide national and military leadership the information needed to accomplish missions, realize national goals and objectives, and implement the national security strategy. During peacetime, intelligence helps commanders identify instability, project future adversary capabilities, make acquisition decisions, protect technological advances, define weapons systems and ISR systems requirements, shape organizations, and design training to ready the joint force and PNs. Intelligence assets monitor foreign states, volatile regions, and transnational issues to identify threats to US interests in time for senior military leaders to respond effectively. Intelligence support is equally critical throughout the range of military operations.

a. **Intelligence Support During Military Engagement, Security Cooperation, and Deterrence Operations.** Maintaining a forward presence enables US forces to gain regional familiarity and develop a common understanding of important cultural, historical, interpersonal, and social differences. Activities such as professional military exchanges, forward basing, and cooperative relationships with multinational partners enhance US forces' ability to shape potential military engagement, security cooperation, and deterrence operations, gain an understanding of multinational tactics and procedures, enhance information sharing, and establish mutual support with host country nationals. Intelligence support is essential to activities such as emergency preparedness, arms control verification, combating terrorism, counterdrug operations, enforcement of sanctions and exclusion zones, ensuring freedom of navigation and overflight, nation assistance, protection of shipping, shows of force, and support to insurgency and counterinsurgency operations. Intelligence provides information on the OE in relation to the JFC's questions concerning actual and potential threats, terrain, climate and weather, infrastructure, cultural characteristics, medical conditions, population, and leadership. Intelligence helps the JFC determine which forces to employ and assists in estimating the duration of the operation. GEOINT that informs the JFC on the spatial and temporal relationships and patterns of the local population and their interactions with the environment supports this process.

b. **Intelligence Support During Crisis Response and Limited Contingency Operations.** Intelligence provides assessments that help the JFC decide which forces to deploy; when, how, and where to deploy them; and how to employ them in a manner that accomplishes the mission. The intelligence requirements in support of crisis response and limited contingency operations such as noncombatant evacuation operations, peace operations, foreign humanitarian assistance, recovery operations, chemical, biological, radiological, and nuclear response actions, and threats or incidents, strikes and raids, homeland defense, and defense support of civil authorities (DSCA) are similar to those required during major operations. During disaster relief operations, intelligence can play an important role in surveying the extent of damage and can assist in planning for the deployment of relief forces. Intelligence is essential to protect joint forces participating in these operations. While intelligence efforts are supporting peacekeeping operations, intelligence should also provide the JFC with warning of any possible escalation of violence and a basis upon which to develop necessary plans and orders. Intelligence professionals providing support for homeland defense and DSCA shall comply with intelligence oversight policies and regulations. Commanders and staffs should carefully consider the legal and policy limits imposed on intelligence activities in support of DSCA, and on intelligence activities involving US citizens and entities. This oversight extends to IAA products. IAA is SecDef approved use of DOD ISR and intelligence capabilities for domestic non-intelligence activities during DSCA missions.

c. **Intelligence Support During Major Operations and Campaigns.** Intelligence identifies enemy capabilities, COGs, and vulnerabilities, projects probable COAs, and assists in planning friendly force employment. By determining the symmetries and asymmetries between friendly and enemy forces, intelligence assists the JFC and operational planners in identifying the best means to accomplish the joint force mission. For example, intelligence provides the JFC and component commanders with information on the relevant physical, informational, and cognitive dimensions of the information environment and their impact on military operations; estimates of what the enemy's information capabilities are; when, where, and how the joint force can exploit its information superiority; and the threat the enemy poses to friendly information and information systems.

(1) Intelligence that enables the JFC to focus and leverage combat power and to determine acceptable risk is key to allowing the JFC to achieve powerful, dynamic concentrations when and where the enemy is vulnerable, and permits the JFC to exploit the maximum range of joint fires. Intelligence provides key elements to targeting by providing identification of HVTs, collection to develop these targets, weapons and platform delivery recommendations, collateral damage estimates, and BDA of the extent of damage to, or effect on, the targets.

(2) Intelligence support to the commander should be anticipatory, timely, relevant, and precise. Intelligence personnel maximize and synchronize support to the commander by focusing on PIRs. The result of the intelligence process should be a product or service that enhances planning, decision making, and assessment.

6. The Role of Intelligence in Military Operations

Intelligence constitutes one of six basic groups of joint functions (related capabilities and activities grouped together to help JFCs integrate, synchronize, and direct joint operations). Other joint functions include command and control, fires, movement and maneuver, protection, and sustainment. Some functions, such as command and control and intelligence, apply to all operations. Others, such as fires, apply as required by the JFC's mission.

a. Intelligence plays a critical and continuous role in supporting military operations. Technology, precise global positioning, and telecommunications provide commanders with the capability to determine accurate locations of friendly and enemy forces, as well as to collect, process, and disseminate relevant data to thousands of locations. These capabilities, combined with the ability to deny or degrade the enemy's ability to collect, process, and disseminate an uninterrupted flow of information, provide the JFC with information superiority. Likewise, the fusion of all-source intelligence along with the integration of sensors, platforms, command organizations, and logistic support centers allows a greater number of operational tasks to be accomplished faster, and enhances awareness of the OE—a key component of information superiority.

b. The most important role of intelligence in military operations is to provide commanders and their staffs with analysis of key aspects of the OE to assist them in their decision-making process. This includes determining adversary capabilities and intentions; identifying adversary critical COGs and vulnerabilities; and estimating the adversary COAs by probability. Visualization of the OE requires a thorough understanding of the characteristics of the operational area and the current dispositions and activities of adversary and neutral forces. It requires knowing the adversary's current and future capability to operate throughout the OE based on a detailed analysis of the impact of weather, geography, and other relevant considerations. Most important, visualization requires understanding the adversary's objectives, identifying how they might fulfill them, and their readiness to achieve them. Together, all these factors make a critical contribution to the JFC's capability to achieve information superiority. However, intelligence must also enable the JFC to know the potential and probable future state of events well in advance of the adversary. Based on this intelligence, the JFC may anticipate adversary actions and plan detailed countermeasures.

c. **Red Teams and Red Cells.** Command red teams are organizational elements comprised of trained, educated, and practiced experts that provide the JFC an independent capability to conduct critical reviews and analysis, explore plans and operations, and analyze adversary capabilities from an alternative perspective. Red teams assist joint operation planning by validating assumptions about the adversary, as well as participating in the wargaming of friendly and adversary COAs. In contrast, J-2 red cells perform threat emulation.

d. **Determining adversary intent is one of the primary challenges confronting intelligence.** The factor that makes analyzing intent difficult is developing judgments based upon the dynamic process of action and reaction between friendly and enemy forces. This process requires the intelligence officer to assess the outcomes of future friendly actions, then simultaneously forecast the following factors: the likelihood of the adversary detecting the action; how the adversary will interpret the action; the adversary's future capabilities; and finally, how the adversary is most likely to react. Moreover, an adversary will often use a deception plan to mislead friendly analysts. A properly trained and augmented red team can reduce the risk associated with long-term prediction of enemy reaction by using red team methodologies designed to analyze the situation from alternative perspectives. These perspectives should be based on knowledge of the adversary's culture, doctrine, capabilities, and other relevant factors.

(1) A simple example of the process of action and reaction is the situation in which an intelligence officer, having detected certain adversary actions and correctly determined the adversary's intent, forecasts that the adversary is preparing to attack. The commander reacts by having friendly forces take appropriate defensive measures. However, the adversary commander detecting these actions decides attacking is no longer a desirable COA, and cancels the attack. In this example, adversary actions produced a friendly reaction resulting in changes to the adversary's intent. This situation is known as the paradox of warning and is depicted in Figure I-8.

(2) Accurate estimates should inform the JFC of the full range of actions open to the adversary and estimate the relative order of probability of their adoption. The confidence placed on the analytic judgments contained in estimative intelligence products helps commanders assess the risks associated in selecting friendly options.

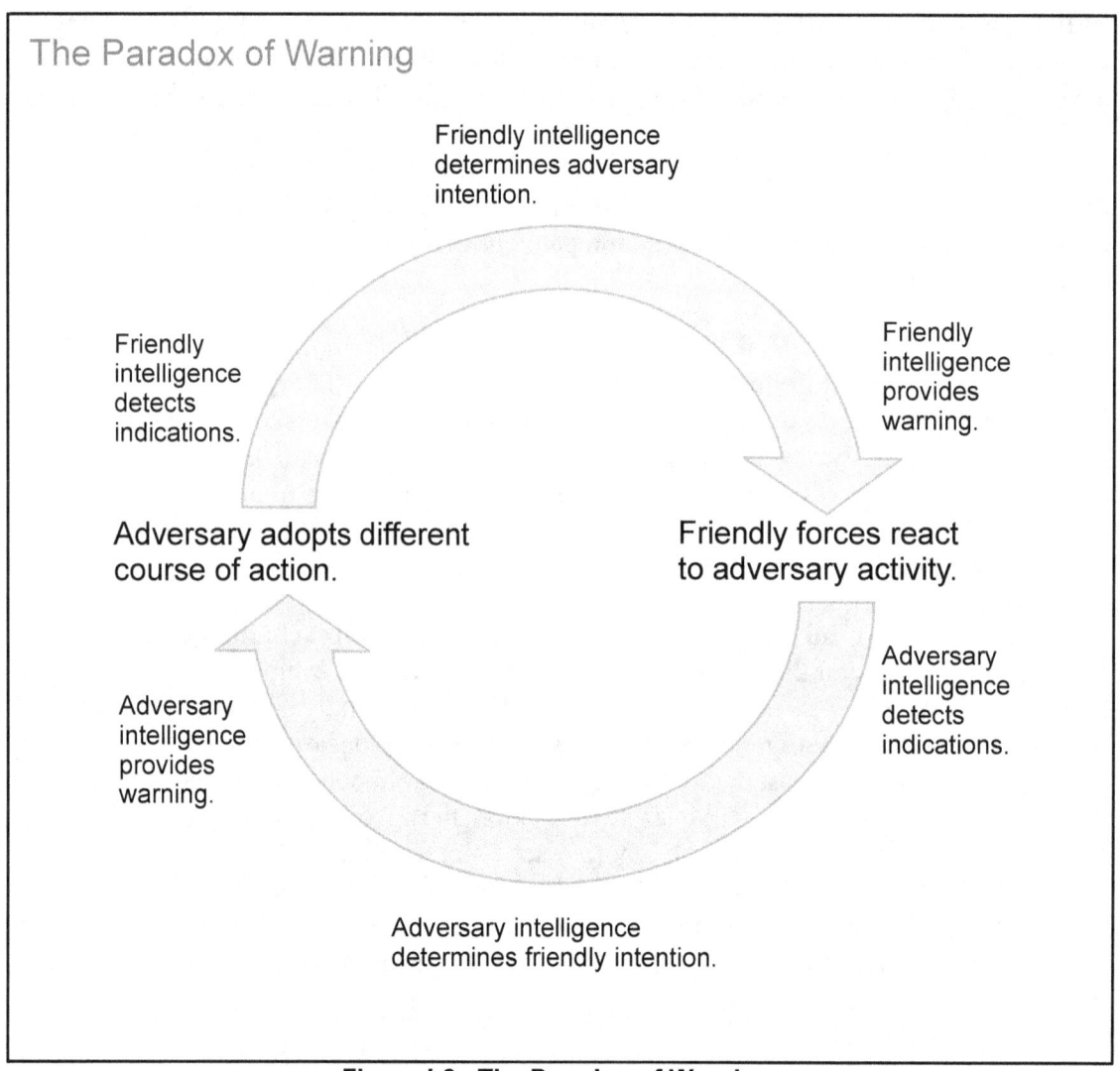

Figure I-8. The Paradox of Warning

Intentionally Blank

CHAPTER II
PRINCIPLES OF JOINT INTELLIGENCE

> *"Tell me what you know...tell me what you don't know...tell me what you think—always distinguish which is which."*
>
> **General Colin Powell, US Army**
> **Guidance to Joint Staff J-2 on 13 November 1992**
> **Chairman of the Joint Chiefs of Staff, 1989-1993**

1. Introduction

This chapter combines intelligence theory and operating experience into fundamental principles that are intended to contribute to effective and successful joint intelligence operations. The following principles for conducting joint intelligence activities are appropriate at all levels of war across the range of military operations (see Figure II-1).

2. Perspective

Intelligence analysts should strive to understand all relevant aspects of the OE. This understanding should include not only the adversary's disposition, but also the sociocultural nuances of individuals and groups in the OE. The JFC should require the J-2 to assess all proposed actions from the following perspective: "How will the adversary likely perceive this action, and what are the adversary's probable responses?" Carrying out these intelligence responsibilities calls for sound judgment as well as expertise.

a. The ability to think like the adversary is predicated on a detailed understanding of the adversary's goals, motivations, objectives, strategy, intentions, capabilities, methods of

---

Principles of Joint Intelligence

- Perspective (Think like the adversary.)
- Synchronization (Synchronize intelligence with plans and operations.)
- Integrity (Remain intellectually honest.)
- Unity of Effort (Cooperate to achieve a common end state.)
- Prioritization (Prioritize requirements based on commander's guidance.)
- Excellence (Strive to achieve the highest standards of quality.)
- Prediction (Accept the risk of predicting adversary intentions.)
- Agility (Remain flexible and adapt to changing situations.)
- Collaboration (Leverage expertise of diverse analytic resources.)
- Fusion (Exploit all sources of information and intelligence.)

Figure II-1. Principles of Joint Intelligence

operation, vulnerabilities, and sense of value and loss. The J-2 should understand the adversary's culture and pertinent actors in the OE. The ability of intelligence analysts to think and react like the adversary and understand sociocultural factors is of particular value during the wargaming of various COAs and the determination of enemy HVTs. Properly trained personnel formed in structured or ad hoc red teams portray the adversary and their most probable or dangerous actions during the war game.

b. Understanding how an adversary will adapt to the environment, conceptualize the situation, consider options, and react to our actions, should be an integral part of a continuing interaction of the intelligence staff with the JFC and other staff elements. This comprehensive understanding is essential to: recognizing challenges to our national security interest; establishing security policy; when appropriate, formulating clear, relevant, and attainable military objectives and strategy; determining, planning, and conducting operations that will help attain US policy objectives; and identifying the adversary's strategic and operational COGs.

> *"Great advantage is drawn from knowledge of your adversary, and when you know the measure of his intelligence and character you can use it to play on his weaknesses."*
>
> **King Frederick the Great of Prussia,**
> **Instructions for His Generals, 1747**

3. Synchronization—Synchronize Intelligence with Plans and Operations

Intelligence should be synchronized with operations and plans in order to provide answers to intelligence requirements in time to influence the decision they are intended to support. Intelligence synchronization requires that all intelligence sources and methods be applied in concert with the OPLAN and OPORD. OPLAN and OPORD requirements therefore constitute the principal driving force that dictates the timing and sequencing of intelligence operations. IP and direction, collection, processing and exploitation, analysis and production, and dissemination should all be accomplished with sufficient lead time to permit the integration of the intelligence product in operational decision making and plan execution. Intelligence evaluation and feedback from commanders, operators, and intelligence personnel must also be accomplished in a timely manner to keep intelligence operations focused to support the commander's plan and intent. Effective synchronization results in the maximum use of every intelligence asset where and when it will make the greatest contribution to success. Intelligence synchronization is the coordination among each type and level of intelligence operation, and the integration of intelligence processes with plans and operations comprises intelligence synchronization.

a. The most common error in attempting to synchronize intelligence with operations and plans is the failure to build sufficient lead time for intelligence production and operational decision making. To avoid late intelligence, the JFC, J-3, and the plans directorate of a joint staff (J-5) in collaboration with the J-2, should establish a suspense or specify a timeframe during which each intelligence requirement must be answered in order to support decision making and operation planning. Likewise, the J-2 must provide sufficient lead time for the collection, processing, analysis, and dissemination of the requisite intelligence to meet the commander's specified deadline. To facilitate synchronization, the J-2 should be involved as early as possible in the operation planning effort and play an active role during the wargaming and analysis of all COAs and plans.

b. The commander drives the intelligence synchronization effort by determining the friendly COA, PIRs, and points in time and space (decision points) where critical events and activity would necessitate a command decision. Decision points are identified on a decision support template developed during the JIPOE process and wargaming. This template provides the basis for PIR development, optimized collection planning, and the formulation of an intelligence synchronization matrix.

4. Integrity—Remain Intellectually Honest

Intellectual integrity must be the hallmark of the intelligence profession. It is the cardinal element in intelligence analysis and reporting, and the foundation on which credibility with the intelligence consumer is built. Integrity requires adherence to facts and truthfulness with which those facts are interpreted and presented. Moral courage is required to remain intellectually honest and to resist the pressure to reach intelligence conclusions that are not supported by facts. The methodology, production, and use of intelligence should not be directed or manipulated to conform to a desired result; institutional position; preconceptions of a situation or an adversary; or predetermined objective, operation, or method of operations. **Intelligence concerning a situation is one of the factors in determining policy, but policy does not determine intelligence.**

a. Intelligence analysts should take active measures to recognize and avoid cognitive biases which affect their analysis. Cognitive bias results when intelligence analysts see the world through lenses colored by their own perceptions and paradigms. Intelligence is filtered through these paradigms and perceptions, and analysts are tempted to fit information into pre-existing beliefs and discard information that does not fit.

b. Intelligence analysts must continuously guard against becoming rigidly committed to a specific interpretation of a set of facts (i.e., they must not ignore or downplay the significance of facts that do not fit a preferred hypothesis or that contradict a previous assessment). Intelligence should be continuously reviewed and, where necessary, revised, taking into account all new information and comparing it with what is already known. Intelligence professionals must have the integrity to admit analytic misjudgments and the courage to change or adjust previously stated assessments when warranted by new information. Intelligence analysts must avoid group think; a mode of thinking that occurs when group members strive for agreement without examining alternatives. By definition, indicators may be assessments that discourage creativity, have no individual responsibility or uncritical acceptance, or are unanimous. Likewise, intelligence analysts must guard against courting favor from superiors by following hypotheses that support established views or a leader's biases and desires.

c. The same integrity and analytic process must extend to reporting what is not known. Intelligence professionals must avoid the temptation to make assessments appear more definitive than may be warranted by the facts. Intellectual integrity requires the intelligence professional to distinguish for the commander those conclusions that are solidly grounded in fact and those that are extrapolations or extensions of the fact. The commander cannot be left with uncertainty regarding what is fact, what is opinion, and what is unknown.

INTEGRITY UNDER PRESSURE

At the outset of the Spanish-American War, Colonel Arthur L. Wagner was head of the Military Information Division (the War Department's embryonic intelligence organization). Driven by public sentiment, President McKinley and Secretary of War Russell A. Alger were determined to attack Spanish forces in Cuba not later than summer 1898. Wagner at once prepared a careful assessment of the Spanish forces, terrain, climate and environmental conditions in Cuba—the basic intelligence needed for operational planning. Wagner's assessment also identified recurring outbreaks of yellow fever in Cuba during the summer months as a crucial planning consideration. At a White House meeting, Wagner recommended postponement of any invasion until the winter months in order to reduce what would otherwise be heavy American losses from the disease. President McKinley reluctantly endorsed his view. As they left the meeting, Secretary of War Alger was furious with Colonel Wagner.

"You have made it impossible for my plan of campaign to be carried out," he told Wagner. "I will see to it that you do not receive any promotions in the Army in the future."

The Secretary of War made good on his promise, for although Colonel Wagner was promoted years later to brigadier general, the notice of his appointment reached him on his death bed. Furthermore, Alger influenced McKinley to reauthorize a summer invasion of Cuba. Fortunately United States forces won a quick victory, but as Wagner predicted, the effects of disease soon devastated the force. The ravages of yellow fever, typhoid, malaria and dysentery accounted for more than 85 percent of total casualties and were so severe that by August 1898 less than one quarter of the invasion force remained fit for service.

According to his peers, Wagner deliberately jeopardized his career in order to satisfy a sense of duty, rather than bow to political pressure. Information that American lives could be saved by avoiding the worst time of the year for yellow fever was more important to him than currying favor with the Secretary of War.

SOURCE: Various Sources

---

5. Unity of Effort—Cooperate to Achieve a Common Objective

Unity of effort is facilitated by centralized planning and direction and decentralized execution of intelligence operations, which enables JFCs to apply all available collection capabilities and PED systems, efficiently and effectively. It optimizes intelligence operations by reducing unnecessary redundancy and duplication in intelligence collection and production. Unity of effort requires intelligence operations, functions, and systems that are coordinated, synchronized, integrated, and interoperable. Intelligence organizations (joint, national, and multinational) operating in a JFC's operational area must have a clear understanding and common acceptance of the command's desired effects, objectives, and end state. This is particularly important when employing distributed, reachback, and federated capabilities, many of which are not forward deployed in a JFC's operational area.

a. Organic and attached intelligence assets operating in the JFC's operational area, as well as national and theater intelligence resources supporting that force should be integrated into an interoperable architecture so that appropriate elements have access to required intelligence. This approach allows the JFC and J-2 to orchestrate pertinent intelligence activities to meet the joint force's intelligence requirements. The seamless provision of joint intelligence support to operational forces as they deploy from one theater to another is particularly important. To effectively plan and execute unit missions, deploying intelligence personnel must know the supported commander's concept of intelligence operations, intelligence architecture, estimate of the situation, map standards, and other specific requirements. This timely information should be provided to deploying forces in a standardized electronic format by intelligence producers. This focuses the ICs effort on satisfying operational requirements.

b. Achieving unity of effort is most challenging during the coordination of multinational operations or when supporting another lead federal agency. Unity of effort in this environment requires establishing an atmosphere of trust and cooperation. It also requires understanding the PNs' requirements, perceptions, and intelligence policies and procedures.

The allocation of high demand, intelligence, reconnaissance, and surveillance resources, such as the RQ-4A Global Hawk, should be based on prioritized requirements.

Unity of effort should maximize the intelligence support provided to the JFC, while simultaneously facilitating information sharing among other appropriate commanders, staffs, and partners or coordinating with the multinational force.

6. Prioritization—Prioritize Requirements Based on Commander's Guidance

Because operational needs for intelligence often exceed intelligence capabilities, prioritization of collection and production efforts, and intelligence resource allocation are important aspects of the IP process. Prioritization offers a mechanism for addressing requirements and effectively managing risk by identifying the most important tasks and applying available resources against those tasks. Implicit in prioritization is the realization that some intelligence requirements are more important than others. Also implicit is a realization that some lower priority requirements might not be accomplished due to resource limitations. Effective prioritization is absolutely dependent upon active cooperation and coordination between intelligence producers and intelligence consumers.

a. Intelligence consumers drive the intelligence prioritization effort by identifying their intelligence needs and the relative importance of those needs. J-2s advise and assist in this effort by recommending intelligence priorities based on the commander's guidance and operational needs. At all levels, the commander's identification of intelligence needs determines prioritization.

b. An agreed upon prioritization framework provides the basis for optimizing the allocation of limited national intelligence resources among CCMDs, and for CCMD collection and PED resources for a subordinate force. The Global Force Management (GFM) process determines the allocation of collection and associated PED resources across the CCMDs based upon the prioritization provided by SecDef. The allocation of national intelligence resources is based upon the National Intelligence Priorities Framework established by the Director of National Intelligence (DNI) and should be consistent with DIAP established priorities and CCMD PIRs. Without clear prioritization and understanding of risk at all levels, competition for ISR resources not only reduces what intelligence could provide, it also inhibits full cooperation among organizations that see themselves as competitors rather than teammates.

c. Military personnel requirements not associated with allocated PED force packages, as well as the collection resources aligned with them, are submitted through RFFs. GFM principles are applied to filling these requirements and result in coordination among force providers and the Joint Staff, and approval by SecDef.

7. Excellence—Strive to Achieve the Highest Standards of Quality

Producers of intelligence should constantly strive to achieve the highest possible level of excellence in their products. The quality of intelligence products is paramount to the intelligence professional's ability to attain and maintain credibility with intelligence consumers. The attributes of intelligence product quality (shown in Figure II-2) are objectives for intelligence activities supporting joint operations and standards against which the quality of intelligence products should be continuously evaluated. To achieve the highest standards of excellence, intelligence products must be:

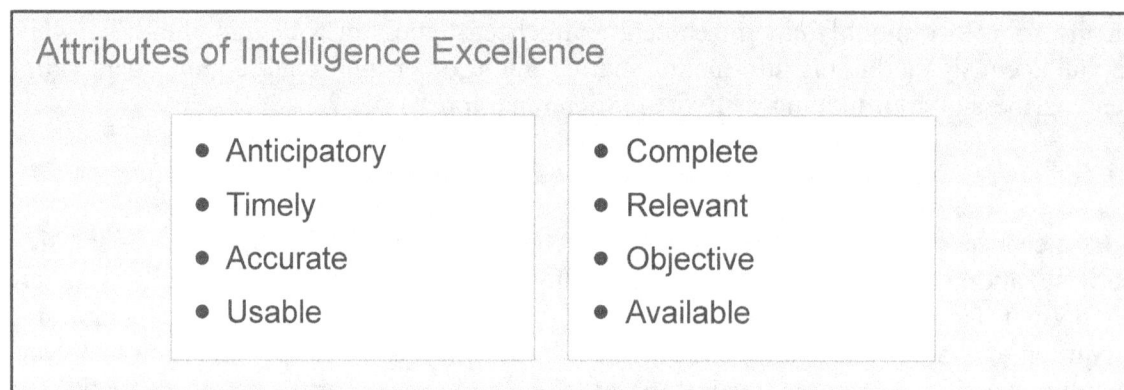

Figure II-2. Attributes of Intelligence Excellence

a. **Anticipatory.** Intelligence must anticipate the informational needs of the commander and joint force staff in order to provide a solid foundation for operational planning and decision-making. Anticipating the joint force's intelligence needs requires the intelligence staff to identify and fully understand the command's current and potential missions, the commander's intent, all relevant aspects of the OE, and all possible friendly and adversary COAs. Most important, anticipation requires the aggressive involvement of intelligence in operation planning at the earliest time possible.

b. **Timely.** Intelligence must be available when the commander requires it. Timely intelligence enables the commander to anticipate events in the operational area. In turn, this enables the commander to time operations for maximum effectiveness and to avoid being surprised. Usually, the need to balance timeliness and completeness should favor timeliness, and if incomplete should be stated in the product, and followed up later. Recognizing and balancing the subtle differences relative to timeliness and completeness is one of the critical art forms for good intelligence.

c. **Accurate.** Intelligence must be factually correct, relay the situation as it actually exists, and provide an understanding of the OE based on the rational judgment of available information. This judgment should evaluate the possibility of an adversary's denial and deception effort. The accuracy of intelligence products may be enhanced by placing proportionally greater emphasis on information reported by the most reliable sources. Evaluate source reliability through a feedback process in which past data received from a source is compared with the "ground truth" (for example, when subsequent events or information confirm the source's accuracy).

d. **Usable.** Intelligence must be tailored to the commander's specific needs, and provided in forms suitable for immediate comprehension. Providing useful intelligence requires its producers to understand the decisions facing the commander, the relevance and impact of intelligence on those decisions, and how to deliver the intelligence to the commander in context so that it balances efficiency and effectiveness. Commanders operate under mission, operational, and time constraints that shape their intelligence requirements and determine how much time they have to study the intelligence provided. They must be able to quickly apply intelligence to the task, and may not have sufficient time to analyze complex intelligence reports. Therefore the "bottom line" must be up front and understandable; oral presentations should be direct; and approved joint terms should be used to effectively convey intelligence.

e. **Complete.** Complete intelligence answers the commander's questions about the adversary and other aspects of the OE to the extent possible, and informs the commander of significant intelligence gaps. To be complete, intelligence must identify relevant aspects of the OE that may impact mission accomplishment or the joint operation execution and offer alternative analysis. Complete intelligence informs the commander of all major COAs that are available to the adversary, and identifies those assessed as most likely and most dangerous. While providing available intelligence to those who need it when they need it, the intelligence staff must give priority to the commander's unsatisfied critical requirements. Intelligence organizations must anticipate and respond to the commander's existing and contingent intelligence requirements by evaluating the intelligence process input and output surrounding the mission.

f. **Relevant.** Intelligence must be relevant to the planning and execution of the operation at hand, and aid the commander in the accomplishment of the mission. It must contribute to the commander's understanding of the adversary and other significant aspects of the OE, but not burden the commander with intelligence that is of minimal or no importance to the current mission. To produce relevant intelligence, the J-2 staff must remain cognizant of the commander's intent and understanding of how the operational concept inflicts desired effects upon the adversary to achieve the military objectives and secure the end state. The J-2 staff must also update requirements as the friendly mission or the adversary situation changes.

g. **Objective.** Due to the decisive and consequential impact of intelligence on operations and reliance of planning and operations decisions on intelligence, it is important for the J-2 to maintain objectivity and independence in developing assessments. When informing the commander, joint intelligence must be vigilant in guarding against biases that shade, slant, or frame assessments to favor the commander's chosen COA or to fit the commander's preconceived notions. In particular, intelligence should recognize each adversary as unique, and avoid mirror imaging while realizing the possible bias involved in their assessment type. For example, current intelligence and warning intelligence estimates may assess the same indicators differently. Red teams can be used to check analytical judgments by ensuring assumptions about the adversary are sound and intelligence assessments help minimize mirror imaging and cultural bias.

h. **Available.** Intelligence must be readily accessible to the commander. Availability is a function of not only timeliness and usability, but also appropriate security classification, interoperability, and connectivity. Intelligence producers must strive to provide information at the most appropriate level of classification and least restrictive releasability caveats, thereby maximizing the consumers' access, while protecting sources of information and methods of collection.

ANALYTIC BIAS: AN ENDURING PROBLEM

1945: "Furthermore, intelligence officers have sometimes been led in extreme cases into pure crystal-gazing attempts to ascertain enemy intentions on the basis of guess or intuition, unsupported by the available evidence... Playing such hunches is not only dangerous in itself; it leads intelligence officers who have committed themselves to guesses of this kind to look for evidence that will corroborate their views and to depreciate contrary indications."

Report of the Committee Appointed by the Secretary of War
to Study War Department Intelligence Activities,
(Lovett Board Report)
5 December 1945

2004: "The Intelligence Community has long struggled with the need for analysts to overcome analytic biases, that is, to resist the tendency to see what they would expect to see in the intelligence reporting. In the case of Iraq's weapons of mass destruction capabilities, the Committee found that intelligence analysts, in many cases, based their analysis more on their expectations than on an objective evaluation of the information in the intelligence reporting."

Report on the US Intelligence Community's
Prewar Intelligence Assessments on Iraq,
Select Committee on Intelligence, United States Senate

8. Prediction—Accept the Risk of Predicting Adversary Intentions

"In my opinion, a commander is not only entitled to a complete analysis of relative enemy capabilities, but to the views of the intelligence officer as to the most likely one to be anticipated, but of course is at liberty to accept or reject those views."

General Walter Krueger
Commanding General, Sixth US Army 1943-1945,
Response to US Army Command and General Staff College Survey on Enemy
Relative Capabilities, 28 July 1948

Although intelligence should identify and assess the full range of adversary capabilities, it is most useful when it focuses on the future and adversary intent. JFCs require and expect timely intelligence estimates that accurately identify adversary intentions, support offensive and/or defensive operations, and predict adversary future COAs in sufficient detail as to be actionable. When justified by the available evidence, intelligence should forecast future adversary actions and intentions. If there is inadequate information upon which to base forecasts, the intelligence staff must ensure that the commander is aware of this shortcoming and that the future contains much uncertainty.

a. The intelligence professional must base predictions on solid analysis using proven tools and methodologies. In conventional analysis, the analyst examines, assesses, and compares bits and pieces of raw information, and synthesizes findings into an intelligence product that usually reflects enemy capabilities and vulnerabilities. However, predictive analysis goes beyond the identification of capabilities by forecasting enemy intentions and future COAs. As discussed earlier, JIPOE provides an excellent methodology for assessing adversary intentions and predicting the relative probability of enemy COAs.

b. Predictive analysis is both difficult and risky (i.e., it challenges the intellectual resources of the analyst while at the same time entailing considerable risk that the events predicted may not come to pass). This type of difficulty and risk apply less to the assessment of adversary capabilities. Predictive analysis is riskier than capabilities analysis because it deals more extensively with dynamic adversary characteristics, a greater range of unknown factors, and possibly enemy deception plans. Therefore, the chances of analytic failure are greater. As a consequence, there may be a tendency among overly cautious intelligence personnel to avoid predictive analysis. However, JFCs need to know enemy intentions as well as enemy capabilities. The analyst who successfully performs predictive analysis and accurately assesses enemy intentions in advance of events performs an invaluable service to the commander and staff.

c. Predictive intelligence is not an exact science and is vulnerable to incomplete information, adversary deception, and the paradox of warning discussed earlier. JFCs must understand that intelligence predictions are only estimates and that they accept an amount of risk in formulating plans based only on the J-2's assessment of the adversary's most probable COA. The J-2 should ensure the JFC is aware of, and has taken into account, all potential adversary COAs and should provide the JFC with an estimate regarding the degree of confidence the J-2 places in each analytic prediction.

9. Agility—Remain Flexible and Adapt to Changing Situations

Agility is the ability to quickly shift focus and bring to bear the skill sets necessary to address the new problem at hand while simultaneously continuing critical preexisting work. Intelligence structures, methodologies, databases, products, and personnel should be sufficiently agile and flexible to meet changing operational situations, needs, priorities, and opportunities. Whether due to military contingencies or diplomatic and/or political challenges, sudden changes in the OE and requirements of intelligence consumers allow little reaction and recovery time. Therefore, the key to successful agility is preparation and organization for all contingencies well in advance. Maintaining responsiveness under such circumstances requires considerable vigilance and foresight. Intelligence professionals must anticipate not only the future decisions of adversaries, but of intelligence consumers as well.

a. Agility is fundamentally a long-term project that requires a principled commitment on the part of JFCs and an accurate vision of future requirements. Agility is built only by prior and continuous preparation. JFCs should continuously strive to increase the competence of the intelligence workforce through prior investment in technical training and professional education. Intelligence organizations should be staffed with people who possess an appropriate mix of skills and personal characteristics that enable them to quickly adapt to, and remain responsive in, a changing OE. Intelligence should employ modularized automated data handling and communications systems that are capable of responding to changing circumstances, facilitating survivability and reliability, and enabling the seamless delivery of intelligence products to consumers regardless of the conditions in the OE. The processes that facilitate these aspects of agility require prior planning and long lead times.

b. Intelligence managers should continuously assess what must be done to support potential requirements, monitor changes in the OE, and adjust resources accordingly. Agility requires anticipation and readiness, but for the most part, intelligence organizations should be managed as if they were already "at war"—staffed, equipped, and organized for flexible responses to changing conditions in the OE.

10. Collaboration—Leverage Expertise of Diverse Analytic Resources

By its nature intelligence is imperfect (i.e., everything cannot be known, analysis is vulnerable to deception, and information is open to alternative interpretations). The best way to avoid these obstacles and achieve a higher degree of fidelity is to consult with, and solicit the opinions of, other analysts and experts, particularly in external organizations.

a. Invaluable expertise on a diverse range of topics resides in governmental and nongovernmental centers of excellence. Likewise, PNs often possess in-depth capabilities in either niche or multiple areas and valuable perspectives on diverse intelligence problems. Without collaboration, intelligence products, and reports end up being one dimensional and thus less comprehensive.

b. Intelligence collaboration relies on unhindered access to and sharing of all relevant information and can take many forms such as competitive analysis, brain storming, and federation. The collaborative sharing of information should not be confused with interorganizational documents coordination; collaboration is informal information sharing among individuals while document coordination is a formal staff process in which official organizational positions are obtained or confirmed. Competitive analysis (in which multiple teams use different or competing hypotheses to analyze the same intelligence problem) is useful if sufficient resources are available. In competitive analysis, it is imperative that each team have access to the same information. In situations where competitive analysis is unfeasible, analysts should brainstorm all possible hypotheses with other analysts to gain different perspectives. Collaboration on complex intelligence problems may benefit from a federated approach in which different organizations may assume responsibility for subtopics within the larger problem. However, in the interest of both unity and simplicity, the joint force J-2 should be the single focal point for assessing and presenting to the commander any disparate intelligence assessments from outside agencies or analysts. The J-2 is responsible for ensuring that the full spectrum of opinions and views obtained through collaboration are considered in the formulation of the joint force's intelligence products.

11. Fusion—Exploit All Sources of Information and Intelligence

Fusion is a deliberate and consistent process of collecting and examining information from all available sources and intelligence disciplines to derive as complete an assessment as possible of detected activity. It draws on the complementary strengths of all intelligence disciplines, and relies on an all-source approach to intelligence collection and analysis. The JFC or J-2 might establish a specific staff organization to conduct fusion analysis.

a. Fusion relies on collection and analysis efforts that optimize the strengths and minimize the weaknesses of different intelligence disciplines. Information is sought from the widest possible range of sources to avoid any bias that can result from relying on a single source of information and to improve the accuracy and completeness of intelligence. The collection of information from multiple sources is essential to countering the adversary's operations security (OPSEC) and deception operations. The operations of all collection sources must be synchronized and coordinated to allow cross-cueing and tipping among collectors. JFCs should develop methods to improve their own and staff's knowledge of the OE. This requires improving the integration of civil information into the planning and operational processes, then sharing that information with external partners to enhance relationships and operational effectiveness.

b. All-source, fused intelligence results in a finished intelligence product that provides the most accurate and complete picture possible of what is known about an activity. While the level of detail in single-source reports may be sufficient to meet narrowly defined customer needs, fused reports are essential to gain an in-depth understanding. Because the adversary will engage in deception efforts, analysts should guard against placing unquestioned trust in a single-source intelligence report. However, if such information is disseminated to meet timeliness criteria, or if no supporting data is available, the single-source nature of the reporting must be made known to the consumers.

LESSON IN FUSION: OPERATION BODENPLATTE

On 1 January 1945, the Luftwaffe conducted an attack (Operation Bodenplatte) against Allied aircraft located on liberated airfields in Belgium. In a postattack assessment, the intelligence staff of the 12th Army Group Headquarters realized they had received adequate signals intelligence (SIGINT) and human intelligence reporting to have provided tactical warning to the commander. The reports, however, had not been fused. Highly compartmented SIGINT (based on Ultra communications intercepts) received before the German attack indicated that an "Operation Bodenplatte" would be launched. However, the SIGINT specialist had no further knowledge regarding this operation or what it entailed. Filed elsewhere in the headquarters, a prisoner of war interrogation report of a former Luftwaffe clerk in Berlin described aspects of Operation Bodenplatte—a plan to employ low-flying aircraft in large numbers. This stove-piped compartmentalization of single source intelligence resulted in the unnecessary destruction of several hundred Allied aircraft.

SOURCE: RAND Corporation,
"Notes on Strategic Air Intelligence in World War II," October 1949

CHAPTER III
INTELLIGENCE ORGANIZATIONS AND RESPONSIBILITIES

> *"The necessity of procuring good intelligence is apparent and need not be further urged."*
>
> **General George Washington,**
> **Letter to Colonel Elias Dayton**
> **26 July 1777**

1. Defense Intelligence and the Intelligence Community

There are a variety of DOD and national intelligence organizations capable of providing support to joint operations. During most joint operations, JFCs will require federated support from the IC to develop a full understanding of the OE. The IC provides analysis of both military and nonmilitary aspects of the OE, as well as the interrelationships which can be depicted in a systems perspective. To efficiently exploit the knowledge and authority of the IC, JFCs and their J-2s should understand the IC roles and responsibilities. This is increasingly important as technology facilitates collaborative analysis and production throughout the IC, thus blurring the traditional distinction between joint and national-level intelligence operations.

a. National Intelligence Leadership Structure

(1) **The DNI** has overall responsibility for intelligence support to the President and the day-to-day management of the IC. Specifically, the DNI establishes objectives and priorities for the IC and manages and directs the tasking of national intelligence collection, analysis, production, and dissemination. The DNI also develops and determines the annual budget for the National Intelligence Program (NIP) and monitors the implementation and execution of the NIP by the heads of IC member organizations. The DNI implements policies and procedures to ensure all-source intelligence includes competitive analysis and that alternative views are brought to the attention of policy makers. Additionally, the Office of the Director of National Intelligence (ODNI) exercises control over the National Intelligence Council, National CI Executive, National Counterterrorism Center, and National Counterproliferation Center, and has authority to establish additional national intelligence centers when deemed necessary to address other intelligence priorities, such as regional issues.

(2) **The Under Secretary of Defense for Intelligence (USD[I])** is the principal staff assistant and advisor to SecDef on all intelligence, CI, and security, and other intelligence-related matters. The USD(I) exercises SecDef's authority, direction, and control over the DOD agencies and DOD field activities that are defense intelligence, CI, security, exercise, planning, policy, and strategic oversight over all DOD intelligence, CI, and security policy, plans, and programs. On behalf of SecDef, the USD(I) coordinates with the Chairman of the Joint Chiefs of Staff (CJCS) to ensure that defense intelligence, CI, and security components within the operating forces (Services and CCMDs) are

resourced to support DOD missions and are responsive to DNI requirements. The USD(I) also provides oversight and guidance for the annual budget for the Military Intelligence Program (MIP) and monitors the implementation and execution of the MIP by the Services and the heads of the CSAs.

(3) **The Director of the DIA** advises SecDef and Deputy Secretary of Defense, CJCS, CCDRs, and USD(I) on all matters concerning military and military-related intelligence and is the principal DOD intelligence representative in the national foreign intelligence process. The Director of DIA also serves in several additional capacities. The Director coordinates intelligence support to meet CCMD requirements and reports to SecDef through the Joint Chiefs of Staff (JCS). As Defense Collection Manager, the Director DIA, serves as the conduit for collection coordination with the joint intelligence operations centers (JIOCs), interagency partners, and ODNI. SecDef-appointed Director, DIA to be the Commander, Joint Functional Component Command for Intelligence, Surveillance, and Reconnaissance (JFCC-ISR). As the Program Manager for the Joint Reserve Intelligence Program (JRIP), the Director, DIA supports activities to leverage joint reserve intelligence centers (JRICs) and Reserve Component capabilities in response to intelligence requirements. Finally, the Director serves as the Defense CI Manager and the Defense HUMINT Manager and is responsible for coordinating all DOD CI and HUMINT resources and requirements.

(4) **The CJCS** provides direction to the Joint Staff Director for Intelligence, J-2, to ensure that adequate, timely, and reliable intelligence and CI support is available to the JCS and the CCMDs.

(5) **The Joint Staff Directorate for Intelligence, J-2,** is a unique organization, in that it is both a major component of DIA (a CSA) and a fully integrated element of the Joint Staff. The J-2 provides continuous intelligence support to the CJCS, Joint Staff, National Military Command Center (NMCC), and CCMDs in the areas of targeting, global warning intelligence, and current intelligence. The J-2 also has the responsibility for coordinating the IP activities of the Services and intelligence CSAs in support of CCDRs. The Joint Staff J-2, ICW other IC elements, provides strategic warning, threat assessments, and intelligence-related advice to the CJCS. It also exercises staff supervision of the intelligence alert center supporting the NMCC and keeps the CJCS apprised of foreign situations that are relevant to current and potential national security policy, objectives, and strategy. During crises, the intelligence support to the NMCC expands as necessary by utilizing DIA assets to form a working group, intelligence task force, or, in the case of a major crisis, an expanded intelligence task force. The Joint Staff J-2 is also responsible for representing and advocating CCMD views and intelligence requirements to the Joint Staff and Office of the Secretary of Defense (OSD). The Joint Staff J-2 is also responsible for coordinating with the CCMDs to staff intelligence-related CJCS orders (e.g., alert orders, planning orders, warning orders) and coordinate RFFs in response to a CCMD request for intelligence capabilities. To staff actions, the joint staff utilizes the Joint Staff Action Process to obtain official CCMD, Service, and intelligence CSA coordination regarding defense intelligence, CI, and security matters affecting the operating forces.

(6) **The Service Chiefs, their intelligence and CI chiefs, and staffs** provide intelligence and CI support for departmental missions related to military systems, equipment, and training. They also support national intelligence activities in support of DOD entities, including CCMDs, subordinate joint commands, and Service components of those commands. Service intelligence staffs and organizations produce a broad array of products and services (such as weapons systems-specific targeting materials) as well as technical expertise in specialized areas such as military information support operations and foreign weapons systems. At both the component and unit level, Service intelligence personnel are involved in the operation of ISR assets and provide tailored intelligence support for weapons system employment.

b. **The IC.** The IC consists of the 17 member organizations (DIA, National Security Agency [NSA], National Geospatial-Intelligence Agency [NGA], National Reconnaissance Office [NRO], Army Intelligence, Navy Intelligence, Air Force Intelligence, Marine Corps Intelligence, Central Intelligence Agency [CIA], Department of State [DOS], Department of Energy [DOE], Federal Bureau of Investigation [FBI], Department of the Treasury, Coast Guard Intelligence, Department of Homeland Security [DHS], the Drug Enforcement Administration, and the Office of DNI). The national intelligence leadership structure is depicted in Figure III-1. Both DOD and non-DOD members of the IC routinely provide support to JFCs while continuing to support national decision makers.

(1) **Military Members of the IC.** The military members of the IC consist of the four defense agencies and the four Service intelligence organizations discussed below. SecDef and USD(I) supervise the DOD portion of the IC and are assisted in their intelligence management responsibilities by the ISR Integration Council and the Military Intelligence Board (MIB). The ISR Integration Council assists the USD(I) with respect to matters relating to the integration of ISR capabilities and the coordination of related developmental activities of DOD components and CCMDs. The MIB serves as the senior "board of governors" for the DOD portion of the IC and works to develop cooperation and consensus on CSA, Service, and CCMD intelligence issues.

(a) **DIA.** DIA has oversight of the DIAP and is the DOD focal point for MASINT, HUMINT, and CI, and is the senior CMA for DOD within the IC, representing all Service and CCMD requirements for national collection. Additionally, DIA analysts provide support in areas such as: all-source military analysis, human factors analysis, counterterrorism, counterproliferation of weapons of mass destruction (WMD), counterdrug operations, information-related capabilities (IRCs), personnel recovery, peacekeeping, and multinational support, noncombatant evacuation operations, warning intelligence, targeting, BDA, current intelligence, systems analysis of the adversary, collection management, intelligence architecture and systems support, intelligence support to operation planning, defense critical infrastructure protection, and DOMEX, BEI, and FEI.

(b) **NSA/Central Security Service (CSS).** NSA/CSS is a unified organization structured to provide for the SIGINT mission of the US and to ensure the protection of national security systems for all departments and agencies of the US Government. Per Executive Order 12333, *United States Intelligence Activities,* the Director NSA is designated as the functional manager for SIGINT.

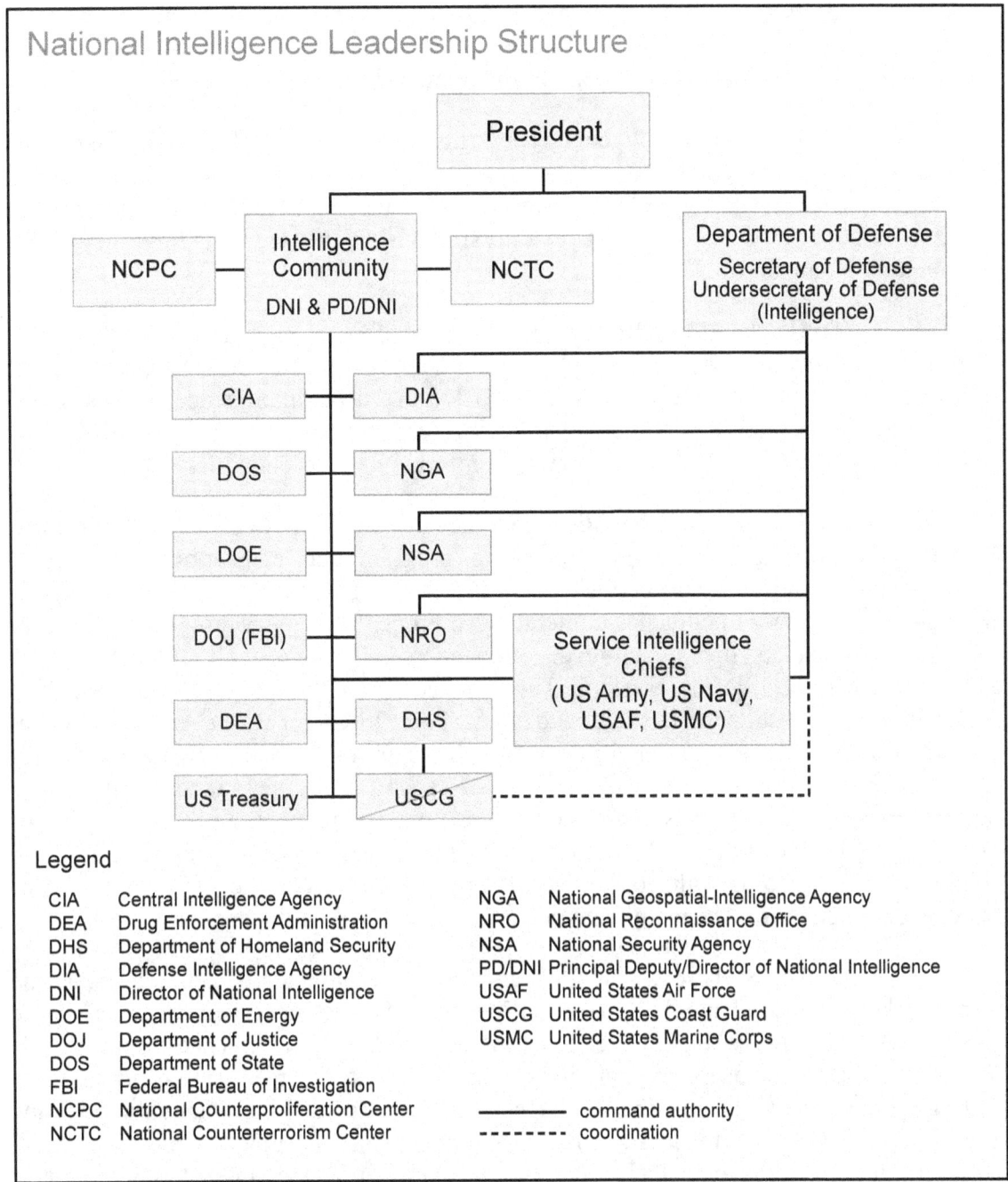

Figure III-1. National Intelligence Leadership Structure

(c) **NGA.** NGA provides timely, relevant, and accurate GEOINT support to include imagery intelligence (IMINT), geospatial information, national imagery collection management, commercial imagery, imagery-derived MASINT, and some meteorological and oceanographic data and information. Per Executive Order 12333, *United States Intelligence Activities,* the Director NGA is designated as the functional manager for GEOINT. See JP 2-03, *Geospatial Intelligence in Joint Operations,* for information regarding the Director's roles and responsibilities as the functional manager for GEOINT and the National System for GEOINT.

(d) **NRO.** NRO is responsible for integrating unique and innovative space-based reconnaissance technologies, and the engineering, development, acquisition, and operation of space reconnaissance systems and related intelligence activities.

(e) **US Army Intelligence.** The Army Deputy Chief of Staff for Intelligence is responsible for policy formulation, planning, programming, budgeting, management, evaluation, and oversight of intelligence activities for the Department of the Army. The Army Intelligence Staff Section exercises staff supervision over the US Army Intelligence and Security Command.

(f) **US Naval Intelligence.** The Director of Naval Intelligence leads the Navy intelligence enterprise and is dual-hatted as the Deputy Chief of Naval Operations for Information Dominance. The Commander, Office of Naval Intelligence reports to the Director of Naval Intelligence and leads the Service intelligence center that focuses on providing intelligence products and services to inform Navy decision makers.

(g) **US Air Force Intelligence.** The Air Force Deputy Chief of Staff for ISR is responsible for intelligence policy, planning, programming, evaluation, and resource allocation and exercises staff supervision over the US Air Force ISR Agency. Through its National Air and Space Intelligence Center, the Air Force ISR Agency provides intelligence support to strategic-and operational-level commanders in the areas of GEOINT, MASINT, SIGINT, HUMINT, OSINT, and technical intelligence (TECHINT), as well as integrated all-source intelligence estimates. In addition to the Air Force ISR Agency, the Air Force enables the use of multiple assets from multiple geographic commands; collecting data across all areas of responsibility (AORs) that may satisfy strategic, operational, and tactical requirements; which may be used by national, joint, or Service specific personnel. The Air Force's globally integrated ISR enables the integration of this collected information to deliver intelligence to the right command at the right time. Lastly, the Air Force Office of Special Investigations is the main focal point for Air Force CI activities.

(h) **US Marine Corps Intelligence.** The Director of Intelligence is the Commandant's principal intelligence staff officer and exercises supervision over the Marine Corps Intelligence Activity. The Headquarters Marine Corps Intelligence Department is responsible for policy, plans, programming, budgets, and staff supervision of intelligence and supporting activities within the United States Marine Corps. The Headquarters Marine Corps Intelligence Department supports the Commandant as a member of the JCS and represents the Service in joint and IC matters. The Intelligence Department has Service staff responsibility for GEOINT, advanced GEOINT, SIGINT, HUMINT, MASINT, CI, and tactical exploitation of national capabilities.

(2) **Nonmilitary Members of the IC.** Joint operations require understanding of both military and nonmilitary aspects of the OE. Much of this expertise falls outside the purview of the DOD members of the IC. JFCs and their J-2s should be familiar with the roles and responsibilities of the following non-DOD members of the IC.

(a) **CIA.** CIA's primary areas of expertise are in HUMINT collection, all-source analysis, and the production of political, economic, and biographic intelligence. Per

Executive Order12333, *United States Intelligence Activities,* the Director CIA is designated as the functional manager for HUMINT.

(b) **DOS.** The DOS Bureau of Intelligence and Research performs intelligence analysis and production on a wide range of political and economic topics essential to foreign policy determination and execution.

(c) **DOE.** DOE analyzes foreign information relevant to US energy policies and nonproliferation issues.

(d) **FBI.** The FBI has primary responsibility for CI and counterterrorism operations conducted in the United States. The FBI shares law enforcement and CI information with appropriate DOD entities and CCMDs. The FBI's Terrorist Explosive Device Analytical Center serves as the lead interagency organization to receive, analyze, and exploit terrorist improvised explosive devices of interest to the US.

(e) **Department of the Treasury.** The Department of the Treasury analyzes foreign intelligence related to economic policy and participates with DOS in the overt collection of general foreign economic information.

(f) **United States Coast Guard (USCG).** The USCG operates as both a military Service and a law enforcement organization and provides general maritime intelligence support to commanders from the strategic to tactical level in the areas of HUMINT, SIGINT, GEOINT, MASINT, OSINT, and CI. The USCG's Intelligence Coordination Center, co-located with the Office of Naval Intelligence, provides all-source, tailored, and integrated intelligence.

(g) **DHS.** The Office of Intelligence and Analysis is a member of the national IC and ensures that information related to homeland security threats is collected, analyzed, and disseminated to the full range of the homeland security customers in the DHS, state, local, and tribal levels, in the private sector and in the IC.

(h) **Drug Enforcement Administration.** The Office of National Security Intelligence collects and analyzes information related to illegal drug production, smuggling, and trafficking.

JP 2-01, Joint and National Intelligence Support to Military Operations, *provides additional information regarding the support that national agencies such as DIA, CIA, NSA, NRO, and NGA, as well as the intelligence and operational organizations of the Services and functional CCMDs can provide to joint forces.*

2. Defense and Joint Intelligence Organizations

In addition to the J-2 staffs at every joint level of command, the key organizations in the defense intelligence architecture are the CCMD JIOCs, the JTF joint intelligence support elements (JISEs), JFCC-ISR, and the JRICs. At the JTF level, a JISE is normally established; however a JIOC may be established at the direction of the JFC based on the scope, duration, and mission of the unit or JTF. **For the remainder of this document**

"JISE" will be used as the standard term to describe the intelligence organization at the JTF level. Working together, these organizations play the primary role in managing and controlling the various types of intelligence functions and operations that comprise the intelligence process described in Chapter I, "The Nature of Intelligence." These organizations are linked by formal relationships that facilitate RFI management, optimize complementary intelligence functions by echelon, and promote the timely flow of critical intelligence up, down, and laterally. In addition to the support provided by joint intelligence staffs and organizations, JFCs receive valuable support from the Service intelligence organizations and from the intelligence staffs and organizations belonging to the joint force components. JFCs should consider the intelligence capabilities of these elements during the planning and execution of all joint operations. Intelligence units and organizations assigned to the joint force will receive at least one intelligence support mission (shown in Figure III-2) from the JFC. Intelligence staffs and forces organic to a component command will remain the assets of that component commander. If the JFC wants the organic intelligence assets of a component to support other components, the JFC will usually assign an intelligence support mission to that component commander.

Support relationships are further explained in JP 1, Doctrine for the Armed Forces of the United States.

a. **The National Joint Operations and Intelligence Center (NJOIC).** The NJOIC is an integrated Joint Staff J-2/J-3/Plans Directorate element that monitors the global situation on a continual basis and provides the CJCS and SecDef a DOD planning and crisis response capability. The intelligence component of the NJOIC maintains an alert center that consists of the Deputy Director for Intelligence, regional desks corresponding to each geographic CCMD, and representatives from each Service intelligence staff element, the intelligence CSAs, and the CIA. The alert center is a continuously manned, all-source, multidiscipline intelligence center providing defense intelligence situational awareness, early warning, and crisis management intelligence support to the President of the United States, SecDef, JCS, CCMDs, deployed forces, Services, and other intelligence consumers during peace, crisis, and war. It provides planning, management, and infrastructure for intelligence working groups and intelligence task forces that provide direct intelligence support during major conflicts. To provide intelligence analytical depth, DIA maintains a 24/7 direct support element at the NJOIC, tailored to the current global situation and operating tempo. The NJOIC coordinates the intelligence response to immediate crises and contingencies.

b. **CCMD JIOC.** The CCMD JIOCs are the primary intelligence organizations providing support to joint forces. The JIOC integrates the capabilities of DNI, Service, CSA, and CCMD intelligence assets to coordinate IP, collection management, analysis, and support. The JIOC construct seamlessly combines intelligence functions, disciplines, and operations into a single organization, ensures the availability of information sources from CCMD, subordinate, and US intelligence resources, and fully synchronizes intelligence with operation planning, execution, and assessment. Although a particular JIOC cannot be expected to completely satisfy every RFI, it can coordinate support from other intelligence organizations. Each CCMD organizes, trains, and directs its JIOC in accordance with the needs and guidance of the CCDR. The JIOC construct is intended to facilitate the agile

---

Intelligence Support Missions

General

An intelligence element in general support will provide support to the joint force as a whole and not to any particular subordinate unit. The intelligence element responds to the requirements of the joint force as tasked by the intelligence directorate of a joint staff (J-2).

Direct

An intelligence element in direct support provides intelligence support to a specific unit. The intelligence element is required to respond to the supported unit's intelligence requirements. As a second priority, the intelligence element will respond to the intelligence requirements of the joint force as tasked by the J-2.

Close

An intelligence element with a close support mission will provide intelligence support on targets and objectives sufficiently near the supported force as to require detailed integration and coordination with the fire, movement, or other actions of the supported unit.

Mutual

Intelligence elements receive a mutual support mission when their assigned tasks, their position relative to each other, and their capabilities allow them to coordinate their activities in order to assist each other to respond to the intelligence requirements of the joint force as tasked by the J-2.

Figure III-2. Intelligence Support Missions

management of all intelligence functions, disciplines, and operations according to the principle of centralized planning and direction decentralized execution.

c. **JTF JISEs.** At the discretion of a subordinate JFC, a JTF JISE may be established during the initial phases of an operation to augment the subordinate joint force J-2 element. Under the direction of the joint force J-2, a JTF JISE normally manages the intelligence collection, production, analysis, and dissemination for a joint force.

See JP 2-01, Joint and National Intelligence Support to Military Operations, *and JP 3-33,* Joint Task Force Headquarters, *for detailed discussion of JIOC and JISE structures, roles, and responsibilities.*

d. **DIA Crisis Response Concept for National Intelligence Support.** In response to crisis and contingency operations, each CCMD must be prepared to provide deployed JTF commanders a means to access national intelligence capabilities and facilitate interaction and coordination among IC participants. This includes providing scalable and dedicated secure communications for reachback into the national IC to leverage all intelligence collection and production agencies. For this purpose, DIA has prepositioned deployable, large-bandwidth, secure satellite communications packages at each CCMD regional support center. Support to JTF commanders should also include forward-deploying CCMD-based IC agency representatives and subject matter experts (SMEs) to support CCMD intelligence operations and facilitate access to their parent agencies. After assessing its capabilities, requirements,

---

and evaluating unfulfilled needs, CCMDs should submit an RFF to the Joint Staff specifically stating manning and/or capability shortfalls. The RFF should specifically identify the skills required from each CSA. Special capabilities can also be requested to close gaps.

e. **United States Strategic Command (USSTRATCOM).** Commander, USSTRATCOM, plans, integrates, and coordinates ISR in support of strategic and global operations and advocate for ISR capabilities. Commander, USSTRATCOM, is the Joint Functional Manager for ISR and associated PED capabilities. JFCC-ISR is a functional component command of USSTRATCOM responsible for executing USSTRATCOM's ISR mission. It develops sourcing solutions for annual and emergent allocation of intelligence collection and associated PED systems to satisfy strategic and high priority CCMD and national operational and intelligence requirements. Allocation of collection capabilities and associated PED systems are staffed through the GFM process to the Joint Staff and approved by SecDef.

f. **JRIC.** A JRIC is an intelligence production and training capability enabling Reserve Component intelligence forces to meet Service components, CCMDs, CSAs, and IC training, readiness, and operational requirements. JRICs are generally located within a Service component-owned, managed, and maintained (Active Component or Reserve Component) sensitive compartmented information facility (SCIF) and surrounding collateral and unclassified areas and use JRIP associated information technology infrastructure and connectivity.

3. Intelligence Federation

During crises, joint forces may also garner support from the IC through intelligence federation. Intelligence federation enables CCMDs to form support relationships with other theater JIOCs, Service intelligence centers, JRICs, or other DOD intelligence organizations to assist with the accomplishment of the joint force's mission. These support relationships, called federated partnerships, are preplanned agreements (formalized in OPLANs, national intelligence support plans (NISPs), or memorandums of agreement) intended to provide a rapid, flexible, surge capability enabling personnel from throughout the IC to assist the CCMD while remaining at their normal duty stations. Federated support can be provided in specific functional areas directly related to the crisis, or by assuming temporary responsibility for noncrisis-related areas within the GCCs' AORs, thereby freeing the supported command's organic assets to refocus on crisis support.

Detailed guidance on intelligence federation planning and support is discussed in JP 2-01, Joint and National Intelligence Support to Military Operations.

4. Command and Staff Intelligence Responsibilities

a. **Joint Force and Component Commander Intelligence Responsibilities.** JFCs and their component commanders are more than just consumers of intelligence. Commanders have key roles and responsibilities in the planning and conduct of intelligence operations. JFCs organize their joint force staff and assign responsibilities as necessary to ensure unity of effort and mission accomplishment. Additionally, commanders (as well as other users) should continuously provide feedback on the effectiveness of intelligence in supporting operations. Figure III-3 depicts commanders' intelligence responsibilities.

(1) **Understand Intelligence Capabilities and Limitations.** Commanders must know intelligence capabilities and limitations as well as procedures and products. Commanders should understand that intelligence analysis provides only estimates to understand the OE, an adversary's probable intention, and COAs—they cannot determine the course of future events.

(2) **Provide Planning Guidance.** Commanders focus the planning process through the commander's intent, planning guidance, and initial CCIRs. The commander's guidance provides the basis for the formulation of PIRs, the concept of intelligence operations, and coherent target development and target nominations.

(3) **Define the AOI.** Commanders should define their AOI based on mission analysis, their concept of operations (CONOPS), and a preliminary analysis of relevant aspects of the OE (prepared as part of the JIPOE process). Commanders should also give clear guidance on the visualization tools and products that support understanding of the OE.

(4) **Specify Intelligence Priorities.** Commanders should specify the PIR component of their CCIRs as early as possible to focus limited intelligence resources. Commanders should not only specify what information is needed, but also when it is needed in order to be integrated into operation planning. Commanders should understand that in some situations, their PIRs will require ISR support from higher echelons that may entail substantial lead time.

(5) **Integrate Intelligence in Plans and Operations.** Commanders are ultimately responsible for ensuring that intelligence is fully integrated into their plans and operations. The successful synchronization of intelligence operations with all other elements of joint

---

Commanders' Intelligence Responsibilities

- Understand intelligence doctrine, capabilities, and limitations.
- Provide planning guidance.
- Define area of interest.
- Specify intelligence priorities.
- Integrate intelligence in plans and operations.
- Proactively engage the intelligence staff.
- Demand high quality, predictive intelligence.
- Protect and promote intelligence integrity and objectivity.

Figure III-3. Commanders' Intelligence Responsibilities

operations occurs in the JIOC and begins with commanders involving their intelligence planners in the earliest stages of the joint operation planning process (JOPP).

(6) **Proactively Engage the Intelligence Staff.** Commanders should actively engage their intelligence officers in discussions of the OE, adversaries, force protection, and future operations. Frequent consultations between the JFC and the joint force intelligence officer facilitates situational awareness and understanding.

(7) **Demand High Quality, Predictive Intelligence.** Commanders must expect their intelligence personnel to provide predictive intelligence that meets the attributes of intelligence excellence. JFCs must also understand the challenges and limitations that confront intelligence personnel in assessing the dynamic OE to include adversary intentions and future COAs thus predictive intelligence is based on incomplete and changing information.

b. **Joint Force J-2 Responsibilities.** The J-2 assists the JFC in developing strategy, planning operations and campaigns, and tasking intelligence assets, for effective joint and multinational operations. Additionally, the J-2 is responsible for determining the requirements and direction needed to ensure unity of the intelligence effort and to support the commander's objectives. The CCMD J-2 provides higher echelons and subordinate commands with a single, coordinated intelligence picture by fusing national and theater intelligence into all-source estimates and assessments. The CCMD J-2's responsibility also includes applying national intelligence capabilities, optimizing the utilization of joint force intelligence assets, and identifying and integrating additional intelligence resources. The scope of needs, resources, and procedures will depend on the mission, nature, and composition of the force. To plan, coordinate, and execute required intelligence operations, joint force J-2s have the following major responsibilities (see Figure III-4).

(1) **Provide Threat Assessments and Warning.** The J-2 is responsible for analyzing all relevant aspects of the OE, determining adversary capabilities, and estimating adversary intentions. The J-2 provides the resulting threat assessments and warning to the joint force and its components in a manner consistent with the intelligence principle of excellence (i.e., the product must be anticipatory, timely, accurate, usable, complete, relevant, objective, and available).

(2) **Participate in all Decision Making and Planning.** Using JIPOE as a basis, the J-2 participates in the JFC's decision-making and planning processes from the time that operations are first contemplated or directed until the completion of the operation. The JFC and the J-2 must conduct a continuous dialogue concerning the adversary's relative strengths, weaknesses, and ability to prevent the joint force from accomplishing its mission.

(3) **Synchronize Intelligence With Operations and Plans.** The J-2 intelligence planners should lead J-2 participation in the pertinent groups to ensure that intelligence activities are synchronized to support the commander's decision-making process and to meet the planners' requirements. This is particularly important in the field of target intelligence, which provides a functional link between intelligence and operations. The commanders' desired effects provide the basis for target development, nomination, and prioritization, while assessment will inform any changes in the commander's objective and strategy.

Joint Force Intelligence Directorate of a Joint Staff Responsibilities

- Provide threat assessment and warning.
- Participate in all decision making and planning.
- Synchronize intelligence with operations and plans.
- Formulate concept of intelligence operations.
- Develop detailed intelligence annexes.
- Integrate joint and national intelligence support.
- Exploit combat reporting from operational forces.
- Organize for continuous operations.
- Ensure accessibility of intelligence.
- Establish a joint intelligence architecture.

Figure III-4. Joint Force Intelligence Directorate of Joint Staff Responsibilities

(4) **Formulate Concept of Intelligence Operations.** To communicate guidance and requirements to higher and lower echelons of command, the joint force J-2 develops and disseminates a concept of intelligence operations. The concept can include such information as tasking authorities, reporting responsibilities, required coordination, obtaining communications-related support and backups, and requirements for intelligence-related boards, centers, and teams.

For further information regarding the concept of intelligence operations, see JP 3-33, Joint Task Force Headquarters, *and JP 2-01,* Joint and National Intelligence Support to Military Operations.

(5) **Develop Detailed Intelligence Annexes.** The JFC's PIRs and the results of wargaming serve as the basis for the intelligence annex of each directed OPLAN and concept plan. The annex will list the JFC's PIRs and the supporting information requirements. It will identify the intelligence forces available for the operation, resolve shortfalls, and assign or recommend tasks (as appropriate) that will best support the joint force's requirements. This annex should allocate available joint force and supporting intelligence assets among the elements of the joint force in accordance with the commander's intent, main effort, and CONOPS. The J-2 must ensure that component intelligence requirements critical to success of key component operations receive appropriate intelligence support. The annex also addresses how any shortfalls between assigned or attached capabilities and requirements will be met by national and supporting capabilities.

(6) **Integrate National and Theater Intelligence Support.** The J-2 should plan for integrating national and theater intelligence elements and products into the joint force's intelligence structure. National and theater intelligence organizations will make

---

operations feasible that could not be accomplished without their access, capability, capacity, or expertise.

Joint and national intelligence support is discussed in greater detail in JP 2-01, Joint and National Intelligence Support to Military Operations.

(7) **Exploit Combat Reporting from Operational Forces.** Forward and engaged combat forces have a responsibility to report information that can be integrated with intelligence obtained from reconnaissance and surveillance assets. In many situations, even negative reporting from operational forces may be valuable (e.g., a lack of contact with adversary forces may be just as significant as positive contact). Likewise, special operations forces (SOF) provide the JFC with a unique manned and unmanned deep look capability, especially useful in areas where other sensors are not available, or cannot provide situational awareness. Based on operational requirements, the J-2 must identify the PIRs and associated reporting criteria to properly focus SOF assets.

(8) **Organize for Continuous Operations.** Intelligence organizations should be structured for continuous day-night and all-weather operations. The J-2's concept of intelligence operations should provide for continuity of support even if communications are severely stressed or temporarily lost. Intelligence resources, activities, and communications must be structured and operated to be sufficiently survivable to ensure required intelligence support is available to the JFC. An important component of survivability is redundancy in critical intelligence architectural components and capabilities.

(9) **Ensure Accessibility of Intelligence.** The J-2 must ensure that intelligence is readily accessible throughout the joint force while still adhering to security standards (e.g., security clearance and need-to-know requirements). All efforts must be made to ensure that the personnel and organizations that need access to required intelligence will have it in a timely manner. When operating in a multinational environment, personnel trained in foreign disclosure regulations should be assigned to the joint force to facilitate the efficient flow of intelligence to authorized multinational members.

(10) **Establish a Joint Intelligence Architecture.** A truly joint intelligence infrastructure must be created to provide the best possible intelligence to the JFC. It must be constructed to ensure protection of information and intelligence from inadvertent disclosure, and guarantee integrity of the data and assured access to all sources. The joint force intelligence architecture required to support the JFC's CONOPS must be designed during the IP process and refined during the pre-deployment phase. JTFs that are primarily composed of forces from a single Service should be provided the necessary personnel and communications to permit the implementation of a joint intelligence system.

Intelligence architecture requirements are discussed in greater detail in Chapter V, "Joint, Interagency, and Multinational Intelligence Sharing and Cooperation."

Intentionally Blank

CHAPTER IV
INTELLIGENCE SUPPORT TO PLANNING, EXECUTING, AND ASSESSING JOINT OPERATIONS

> *"What is called 'foreknowledge' cannot be elicited from spirits, nor from gods, nor by analogy with past events, nor from calculations. It must be obtained from men who know the enemy situation."*
>
> **Chinese General and Tactician Sun Tzu, *The Art of War*, 400-320 BC**

SECTION A. INTELLIGENCE PLANNING

1. Overview

The planning of joint operations is accomplished through the APEX system. The intelligence component of APEX is the IP process and it is conducted by the organizations within the DOD component of the IC. IP procedures are fully integrated and synchronized with joint operation planning and apply to deliberate and crisis action planning. The IP process is a methodology for coordinating and integrating available defense intelligence capabilities to meet CCDR intelligence requirements. It ensures that prioritized intelligence support is aligned with CCDR objectives for each phase of an operation. The DOD portion of the IC develops products that are used by the joint force J-2 to provide the JFC and staff with situational understanding of the OE.

   a. **Dynamic Threat Assessment (DTA) or Theater Intelligence Assessment (TIA).** The DTA is a defense strategic intelligence assessment developed by DIA, which identifies the capabilities and intentions of adversaries for top-priority plans. DIA produces and provides the CCMD an updated DTA prior to mission analysis and updates DTAs as strategic factors in the OE change. For theater campaign plans, DIA produces a TIA. The TIA is a theater-wide defense strategic intelligence assessment that is scoped in accordance with the actors of concern with particular emphasis on how these actors are affected by the strategic environment. These DIA-produced strategic intelligence assessments enable development of the CCMD intelligence staff estimate in order to conduct mission analysis and develop COAs.

   b. **NISP.** The NISP is a supporting plan to a CCMD plan that details how the intelligence capabilities of CSAs, Services, and other DOD Intelligence Enterprise organizations will be employed to meet the CCDR's stated intelligence requirements. It facilitates the integration of theater and national intelligence capabilities and synchronizes intelligence operations. The NISP contains annexes from applicable defense intelligence agencies/organizations that detail their concept for function support.

For additional information on IP, refer to CJCSM 3314.01, Intelligence Planning, *and JP 2-01,* Joint and National Intelligence Support to Military Operations.

SECTION B. JOINT OPERATION PLANNING

2. Joint Operation Planning

a. Joint operation planning encompasses a number of elements, including three broad **operational activities,** four **planning functions,** and a number of related **products** (see Figure IV-1). Each of these planning functions will include as many in progress reviews (IPRs) as necessary to complete the plan. IPR participants are based on the initiating authority or level. IPRs constitute a disciplined dialogue among strategic leaders (most notably the CCDRs, CJCS, SecDef, and, when approved, senior DOS and other key department and agency leadership or their representatives) to shape the plan as it is developed.

b. During JOPP, CCMD J-2s lead development of annex B (Intelligence). Annex B is the intelligence annex to a plan or order that provides detailed information on the adversary situation, establishes priorities, assigns intelligence tasks, identifies required intelligence products, requests support from higher echelons, describes the concept of intelligence operations, and specifies intelligence procedures. The joint force J-2 products normally include but are not limited to the following: a description of the operational area; an evaluation of the adversary; identification of adversary COGs; prioritized adversary COAs; event templates; named AOIs and target AOIs; a decision support template; wargame support; and an intelligence synchronization matrix.

For additional information on JOPP, refer to JP 5-0, Joint Operation Planning, *and JP 2-01,* Joint and National Intelligence Support to Military Operations.

SECTION C. THE INTELLIGENCE PLANNING PROCESS

3. Intelligence Planning Lines of Effort

Joint and national intelligence activities help identify and monitor threats to national security that inform the development of policy and the DOD's overall planning efforts. Through joint operation planning, intelligence priorities are further refined to focus the employment of limited DOD intelligence resources. Thus, IP activities are generally organized along two lines of effort (LOEs): providing intelligence support to joint operation planning and planning intelligence operations as illustrated in Figure IV-2.

a. **IP LOE # 1: Providing Intelligence Support to Joint Operation Planning.** IP activities along this LOE include the production of intelligence assessments and estimates of adversary intentions, capabilities, and COAs. Specific outputs of this LOE are the DIA-produced DTA, or TIA, and the development of tailored products from the CCMD's JIPOE process that culminate in the production and maintenance of the intelligence estimate. These finished intelligence products are disseminated to inform joint operation planning and the development of the commander's estimate through which CCDRs provide SecDef with military options to meet strategic objectives. Activities along this LOE are continuous and typically conducted in parallel with and in support of the CCMD's operation planning and assessment.

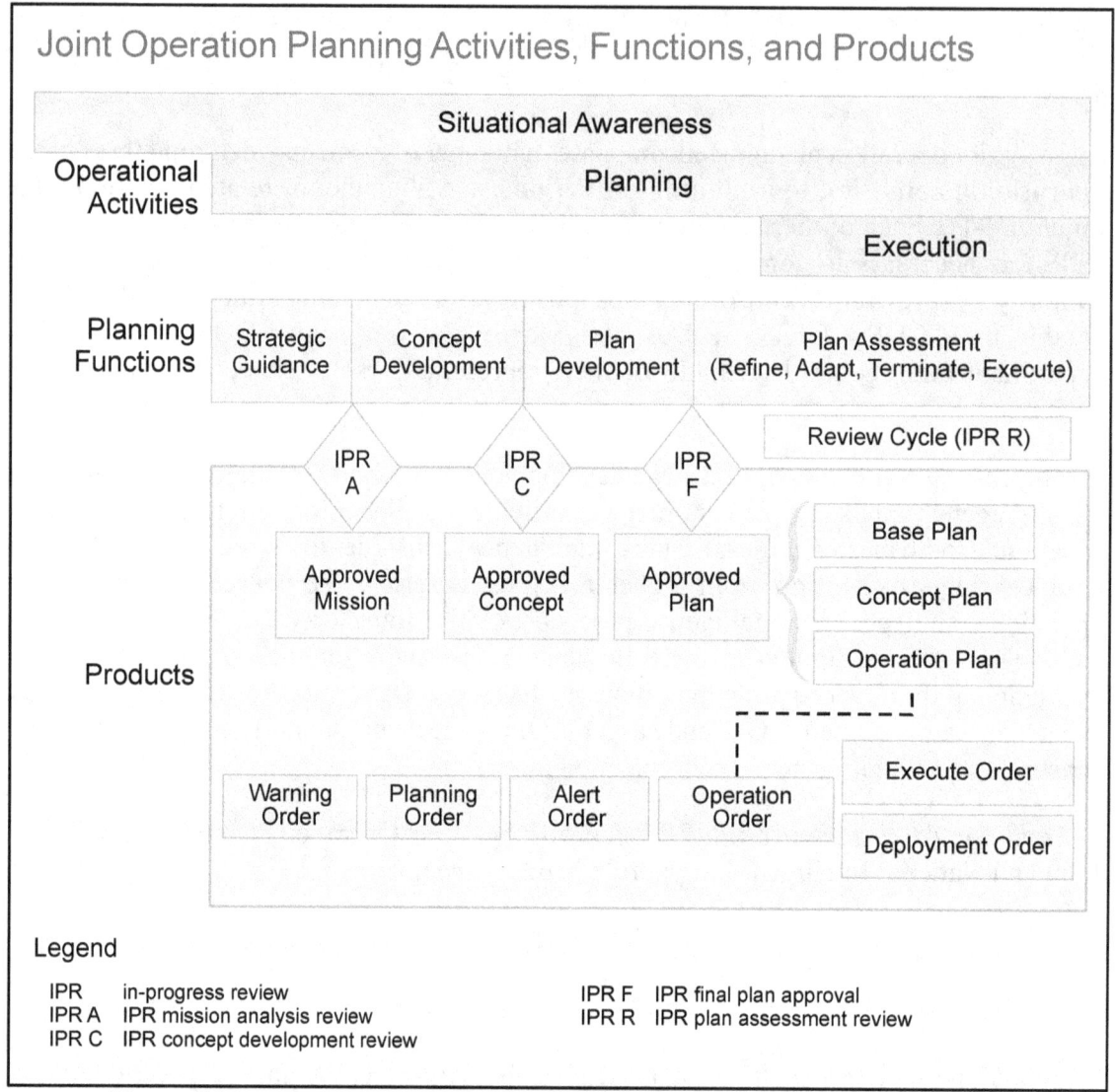

Figure IV-1. Joint Operation Planning Activities, Functions, and Products

b. **IP LOE # 2: Planning Intelligence Operations.** IP activities along this LOE include identifying information gaps, prioritizing intelligence requirements, developing federated production and integrated collection plans, and assessing intelligence capabilities for the purpose of identifying shortfalls and mitigation strategies. Specific outputs of this LOE are the CCMD J-2 staff estimate, which identifies available CCMD intelligence capabilities and anticipated shortfalls, CSA and Service intelligence center estimates, the annex B (Intelligence) to a campaign or a contingency plan, and when appropriate an NISP or the joint intelligence posture assessment. Additional outputs of this LOE may include intelligence resource demand signals that may be articulated through the CCDR's integrated priorities list or RFF. Activities along this LOE are also continuous and are typically conducted internal to the command JIOC as facilitated by an intelligence planning team (IPT), or through the IP steering group ICW the Joint Staff J-2 to facilitate the integration of national-level intelligence support.

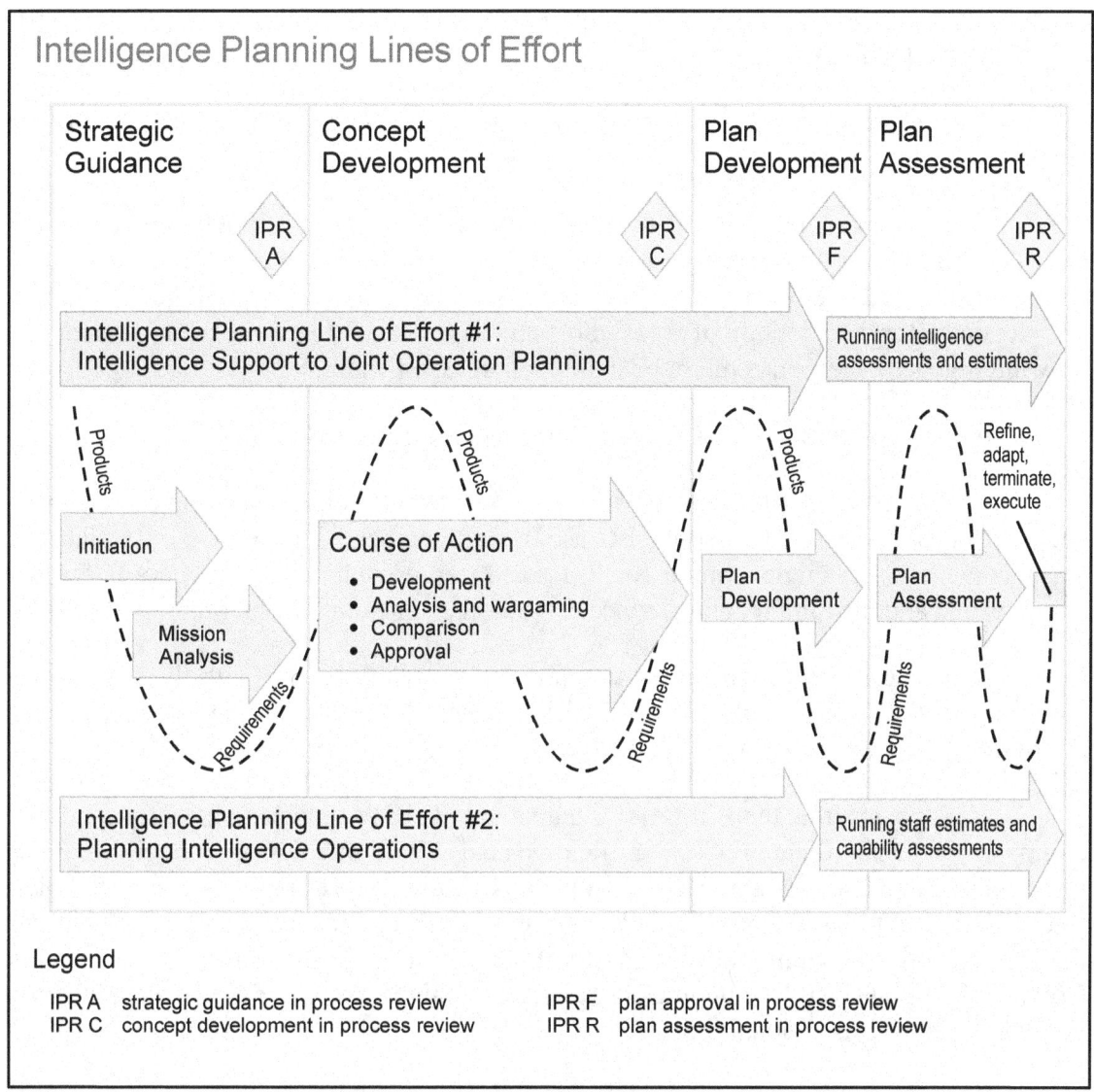

Figure IV-2. Intelligence Planning Lines of Effort

4. Intelligence Planning Activities During Strategic Guidance

a. IP activities along IP LOE # 1: Intelligence Support to Joint Operation Planning

(1) DIA will validate, update, or produce a DTA or a TIA.

(2) At the CCMD level and below, intelligence planners orchestrate the command's continuous JIPOE effort for analysts to provide a baseline assessment of the OE, adversary capabilities, COGs, vulnerabilities and estimated adversary COAs. The analytical cell of the CCMD JIOC evaluates relevant databases and intelligence holdings to identify gaps relevant to the planning effort under consideration. This includes the status of targeting information. The J-2 may form a JIPOE coordination cell to draw relevant information from other staff elements, IC representatives, and PNs as appropriate, as well as request tailored products from the defense IC. The JIPOE process culminates with the production of an intelligence

estimate which is incorporated into the plan as appendix 11 (Intelligence Estimate) to annex B (Intelligence).

For more information on JIPOE, refer to JP 2-01.3, Joint Intelligence Preparation of the Operational Environment.

(3) As core members of the joint planning group (JPG), intelligence planners contribute to the overall plan design and nominate operations objectives, desired effects and other mission success criteria. In nominating mission success criteria, intelligence planners also advocate for the adoption of measurable and achievable objectives while considering how intelligence capabilities might be employed to assess them.

b. **IP activities along IP LOE # 2: Planning Intelligence Operations**

(1) Intelligence planners assemble an IPT or similar community of interest with all-source analysts and collection strategists as its core members (Figure IV-3). Intelligence systems architects, single source analysts and representatives from CSAs, Service components, and the joint reconnaissance center (JRC) may also collaborate with the IPT.

(2) The IPT develops an IP timeline that is synchronized with the command's planning timeline. This ensures tailored JIPOE products, the *initial* intelligence estimate and the *initial* J-2 staff estimate are developed to meet the JPG's requirements.

(3) To generate the J-2 staff estimate, the IPT, ICW representatives from Service component and subordinate JFCs, identifies and analyzes all intelligence capabilities under combatant command (command authority) available to support the execution of the plan. For contingency plans, this may include all assigned and apportioned forces. For ongoing operations and campaign plans this may include all assigned and allocated forces. Conducting this analysis for ongoing operations, campaigns, and crisis action planning, may inform requests for additional forces.

(4) The IPT evaluates current theater collection and production postures to identify available assets that may need to be redirected to support the planning effort or the execution of the plan under consideration. In collaboration with the CCMD's collection managers, joint force counterintelligence and human intelligence staff element (J-2X), the JRC, and representatives from JFCC-ISR, the IPT conducts a preliminary assessment of available collection assets and capabilities. In collaboration with the CCMD production manager, and representatives from the JIOC's analytical cell, the IPT performs an initial assessment of available analytic capabilities.

(5) Based on the list of all available intelligence capabilities, the IPT drafts and submits the *initial* J-2 staff estimate to the JPG to support the command's overall force structure analysis. In addition to listing all available intelligence capabilities, the initial J-2's staff estimate identifies all factors that may affect the employment of these capabilities. Factors such as logistical supportability, basing rights, communications and intelligence systems architecture, linguist availability, and legal restrictions should be considered. Certain employment limitations can be mitigated during COA development ICW the JPG. Other limitations however, may require mitigation through friendly actions outside the

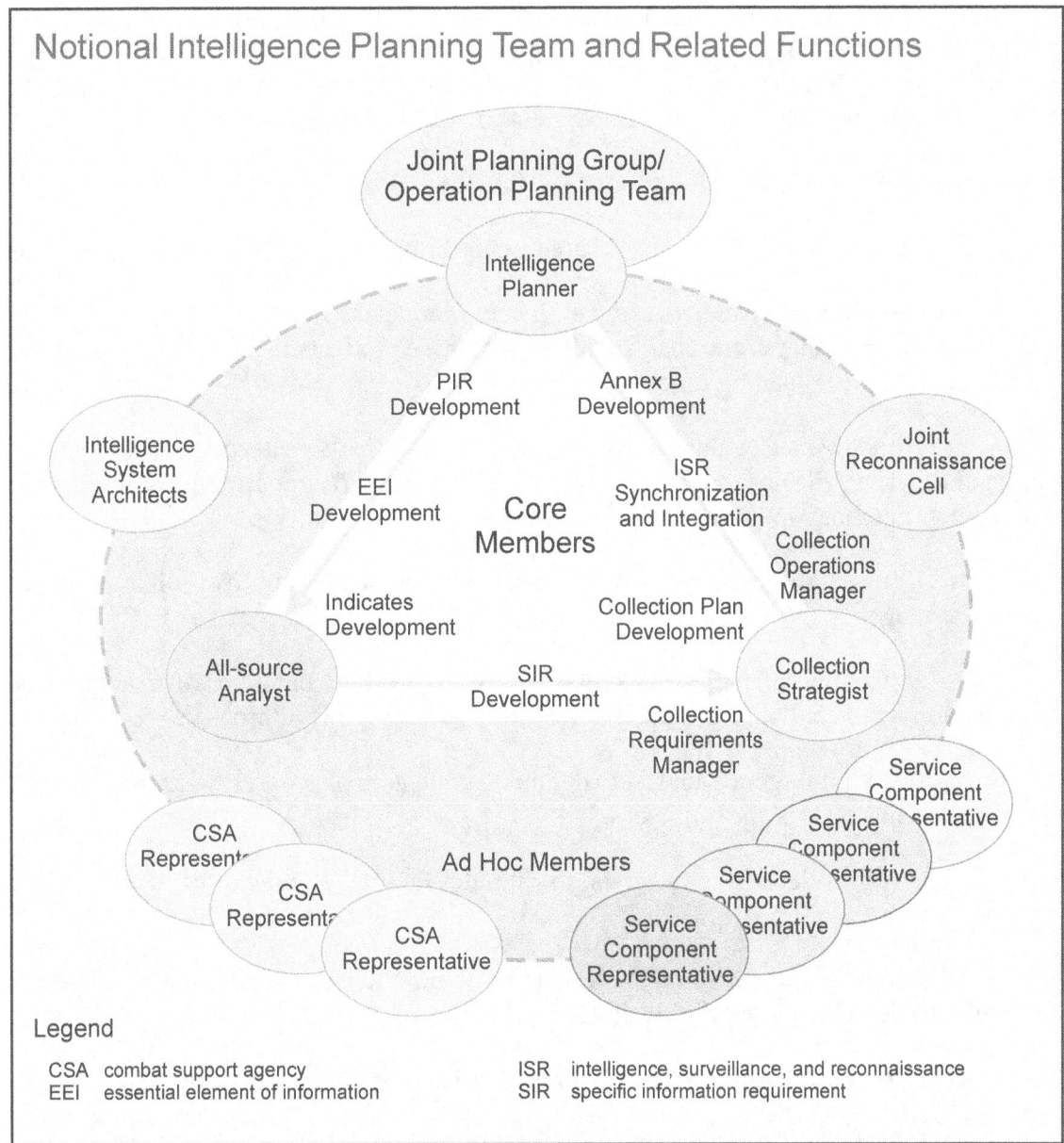

Figure IV-3. Notional Intelligence Planning Team and Related Functions

immediate control of the command. In these instances, intelligence planners in collaboration with the JPG, may nominate appropriate planning assumptions. To validate these planning assumptions prior to COA approval, they may nominate *initial* FFIRs. If left unanswered prior to plan development, *initial* FFIRs, may be included as part of the final CCIRs to be monitored during plan assessment to inform refine, adapt, terminate, execute (RATE) decisions.

(6) Considering all of the identified intelligence gaps relevant to the planning effort and recognizing the uncertainties in analytical conclusions, intelligence planners in collaboration with the JPG, may nominate additional planning assumptions and *initial* PIRs

for validation during the current planning cycle. Upon approval by the J-2 and the CCDR, *initial* PIRs are then passed to the IPT or appropriate mission managers for action. If left unanswered prior to plan development, *initial* PIRs, may be included as part of the final CCIRs to be monitored during plan assessment to inform RATE decisions.

5. Intelligence Planning Activities During Concept Development

a. IP activities along IP LOE # 1: Intelligence Support to Joint Operation Planning

(1) Intelligence planners evaluate JIPOE products to be disseminated to the JPG. The intelligence planner or the analyst will present these products to the JPG in accordance with the established planning timeline.

(2) Intelligence planners coordinate personnel to participate in COA analysis and wargaming. The J-2 may employ multiple representatives to support the JPG during the wargame. These may include:

(a) Intelligence planner to develop and analyze the overall intelligence support strategy.

(b) Red cell personnel to play the role of an uncooperative adversary and red team personnel to challenge planning assumptions and provide alternative viewpoints.

(c) Intelligence analyst to nominate indicators of progress or regression used in the command's assessment process.

(d) Collection strategists to initiate the development of a supporting collection plan.

(3) Intelligence planners will determine intelligence governing factors and highlight the advantages and disadvantages of each COA.

b. IP activities along IP LOE # 2: Planning Intelligence Operations

(1) During COA development, intelligence planners consider how theater intelligence assets and external intelligence resources could be employed to support the execution of the plan.

(2) Based on potential adversary reactions evaluated during COA analysis and wargaming, the intelligence planner and the collection strategist determine how the various collection disciplines could be employed to monitor relevant indicators.

(3) The intelligence planner revises the J-2 staff estimate capturing additional factors, unique to each of the proposed friendly COAs, which may limit the employment of intelligence capabilities. Once identified, the intelligence planner ensures these factors are considered during COA comparison.

(4) The intelligence planner consolidates final PIR nominations from across the staff and drafts PIRs as required to support CCDR decisions. During COA approval, the intelligence planner recommends PIRs through the J-2 for CCDR approval. PIR nominations not approved by the CCDR are processed at a lower priority and satisfied when intelligence resources become available.

(5) Following COA approval, the intelligence planner in collaboration with the IPT develops EEIs and associated indicators required to satisfy the PIR. To maximize support to the commander's operational objectives, the IPT integrates and reconciles these requirements with MOEs and their associated indicators.

(6) Based on intelligence requirements (to include PIRs), information requirements (to include EEIs), their associated indicators, and anticipated SIRs, the IPT then generates a matrix of anticipated production requirements to guide the development of federated production plans and a matrix of anticipated collection requirements to guide the development of integrated collection plans.

(7) The J-2 staff estimate process culminates with the collection and production capability assessments performed against anticipated requirements entered on the collection and production requirements matrices.

(8) The CCMD J-2 will determine whether a NISP is required and will request IP support from the Joint Staff J-2 to initiate NISP development, based on the CCMD J-2 staff estimate, and in accordance with CJCSI 3110.02, *Intelligence Planning Objectives, Guidance, and Tasks*. The Joint Staff J-2 is responsible for publishing a message announcing the NISP effort and requesting points of contact from the relevant communities of interest. Development of the NISP is based on the supported CCMD's PIRs, EEIs, concept of intelligence operations, production and collection requirements matrices, and the J-2's staff estimate of available capabilities to satisfy its requirements. Collaboration between the CCMD, Joint Staff J-2, CSAs, and Service intelligence centers is encouraged and can occur at any time during the planning process. However, the NISP process begins in earnest when the CCMD J-2 judges that the supported plan is sufficiently developed and that requirements matrices are ready for submission to the Joint Staff J-2.

6. Intelligence Planning Activities During Plan Development

a. IP activities along IP LOE # 1: Intelligence Support to Joint Operation Planning

(1) The JIOC's analytical cell completes the intelligence estimate. Selected portions of the intelligence estimate are used to complete the enemy situation paragraphs throughout the plan.

Refer to CJCSM 3130.03, Adaptive Planning and Execution (APEX) Planning Formats and Guidance, *for a complete intelligence estimate format.*

(2) The CCMD J-2 may also provide analytical support and input to other portions of the plan to include annex H, (Meteorological and Oceanographic Operations, and other annexes as required.

b. IP activities along IP LOE # 2: Planning Intelligence Operations

(1) Intelligence planners develop the base annex B (Intelligence) which outlines the intelligence mission, concept of intelligence operations, PIRs, and guidance for how collection, processing and exploitation, analysis and production, dissemination and integration, and evaluation and feedback will be performed during execution. The annex B (Intelligence) also specifies tasks to subordinate intelligence organizations and requirements for external support.

(2) Intelligence planners evaluate whether targeting is necessary to accomplish the operation. If so, the IPT facilitates TSA, target development, and target list management.

(3) Intelligence planners collaborate with discipline-specific managers and other SME to develop required functional appendices to annex B (Intelligence) (i.e., J-2X for appendix 3, [Counterintelligence]).

(4) To ensure the collection plan is fully integrated and synchronized with the contemplated operation, intelligence planners and collection strategists contribute to other portions of the plan such as appendix 9 (Reconnaissance) to annex C (Operations); annex S (Special Technical Operations); and other annexes as required.

(5) If the contingency plan will be supported by a NISP, the Joint Staff J-2 and CCMD J-2 will collaborate to lead the NISP development, production, completion, staffing, and approval process.

For additional information on NISP development, IP support to campaign plans and crisis action planning, refer to CJCSM 3314.01, Intelligence Planning.

SECTION D. PLAN ASSESSMENT AND EXECUTION

7. Intelligence Support to Plan Assessment and Decision Making

Continuous and timely assessments are essential to measure progress of the joint force toward mission accomplishment (see Figure IV-4). Commanders continuously assess the OE and the progress of their campaigns, and then compare them to their initial vision and intent. Commanders and their staffs determine relevant assessment actions and measures during planning. They consider assessment measures as early as mission analysis, and include assessment measures and related guidance in commander and staff estimates. They use assessment considerations to help guide operational design in order to improve the sequence and type of actions along lines of operation. During execution, they continually monitor progress toward accomplishing tasks, creating effects, and achieving objectives. Assessment requirements, and the collection and analytic resources required to perform them are built into plans and monitored. Plans for intelligence collection and analytic support to execution and continuous plan assessment are based on the supported CCMD's anticipated requirements reflected in appendix 1 (Priority Intelligence Requirements) to annex B (Intelligence) of the order. During execution, preplanned collection and production requirements may change in response to dynamic changes to the CCDR's PIRs.

a. Assessment actions and measures help commanders adjust operations and align future operations strategic and operational-level assessment efforts concentrate on broader tasks, effects, objectives, and progress toward the end state, while tactical-level assessment focuses on task accomplishment. Even in operations that do not include combat, assessment of progress is just as important and can be more complex than traditional combat assessment. Normally, the joint force J-2 assists the J-3 or J-5 in coordinating assessment activities.

b. The joint force J-2, through the CCMD JIOC, assesses adversary capabilities, vulnerabilities, and intentions, and monitors the OE. The J-2 helps the commander and staff decide what aspects of the OE to measure and how to measure them to determine progress toward accomplishing a task, creating an effect, or achieving an objective. Intelligence personnel use the JIPOE process to provide JFCs and their staffs with a detailed understanding of the adversary and other relevant aspects of the OE.

c. Intelligence personnel in the CCMD JIOC provide objective assessments to planners that gauge the overall impact of military operations against adversary forces as well as provide an assessment of likely adversary reactions and counteractions. The CCDR and subordinate JFCs should establish an assessment management system that leverages and synergizes the expertise of operations and intelligence staffs.

d. The assessment process is continuous and linked to the CCIR process by the commander's need for timely information and recommendations to make decisions during all phases of the operation or campaign as shown in Figure IV-4. Intelligence support to plan assessment applies during shape as well as execution phases. By supporting assessments of the impacts of shaping activities, the J-2 supports decisions to refine or adapt the campaign plan or to refine, adapt, or terminate contingency plans. During execution, the J-2 continues to provide support to assessments to inform fragmentary order development reflecting decisions to refine, adapt, or terminate ongoing military operations. Intelligence assessments of the current situation provide the means for intelligence analysts to draw conclusions of a potential future situation and estimate the next series of adversary COAs. In so doing, analysts revise and maintain a running intelligence estimate to facilitate continuous planning across multiple timeframes during the conduct of operations.

8. Intelligence Support to the Assessment Process

a. The assessment process uses MOPs to evaluate task performance at all levels of war, and MOEs to determine progress of operations toward achieving objectives. MOPs are used to measure task accomplishment, and answer the question "was the action taken, were the tasks completed to standard?" to produce the desired effect. MOEs are used at the strategic, operational, and tactical-level-intelligence staffs to assess changes in adversary behavior, capabilities, or the OE. MOEs help answer questions like: "are we doing the right things, are our actions producing the desired effects, or are alternative actions required?" Well-devised measures can help the commanders and staffs understand the causal relationship between specific tasks and desired effects.

b. Both MOPs and MOEs can be quantitative or qualitative in nature, but meaningful quantitative measures are preferred because they are less susceptible to subjective

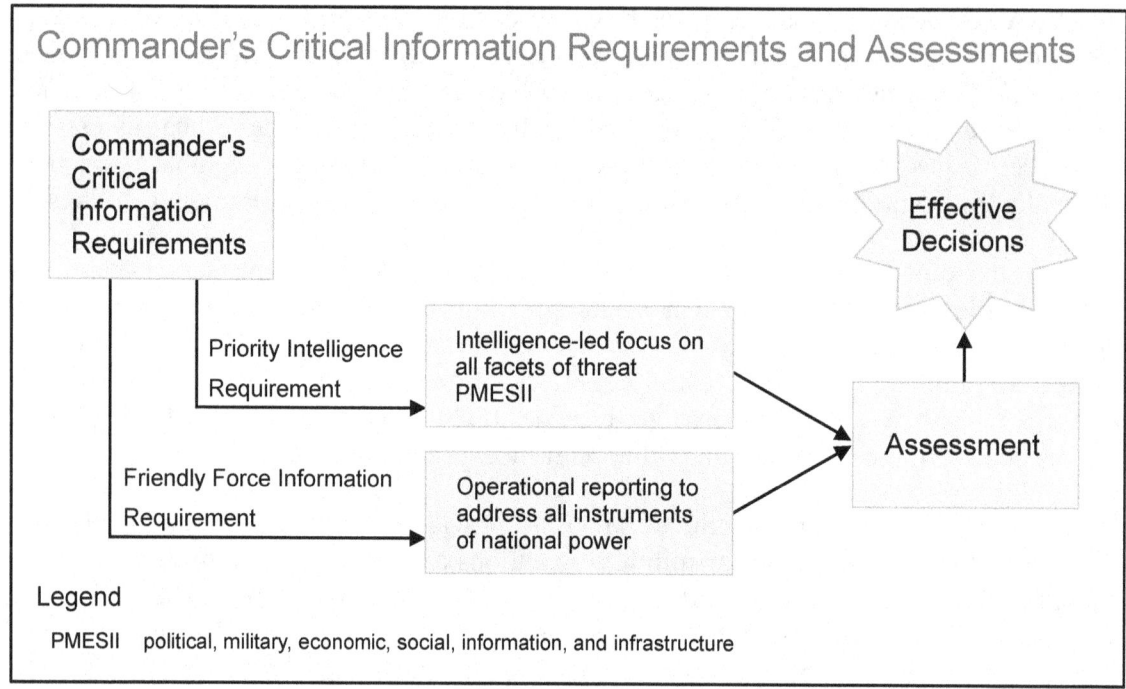

Figure IV-4. Commander's Critical Information Requirements and Assessments

interpretation. Through these measures, the J-2 and the J-3 assist the commander in determining if military operations are producing desired or undesired effects, when objectives have been achieved and when unforeseen opportunities can be exploited or require a change in planned operations to respond to unforeseen adversary actions.

c. MOE assessment is implicit in steps 1, 2, and 3 of the JIPOE process. By continuously performing JIPOE, intelligence analysts have the ability to compare the baseline intelligence estimate used to inform the plan with the current situation and facilitate continuous planning during execution. MOE assessment is informed through the detection of observable or collectable indicators that provide evidence that certain conditions exist. Several indicators may make up an MOE, just like several MOEs may assist in measuring progress toward achievement of an objective. Indicators may be either favorable or unfavorable. While favorable indicators reflect progress towards the achievement of an objective, unfavorable indicators reflect regression and could provide warning of a potential crisis and the need to execute a branch plan, see Figure IV-5.

d. Indicators are developed through the JIPOE process and detected through intelligence disciplines and friendly unit reports (e.g., mission reports or situation reports). Friendly unit reports are used in most aspects of combat assessment, since they typically offer specific, quantitative data, or a direct observation of an event to determine accomplishment of tactical tasks.

For more information on the relationships between the CCIR process, and the assessment process, and continuous planning during execution, refer to JP 5-0, Joint Operation Planning.

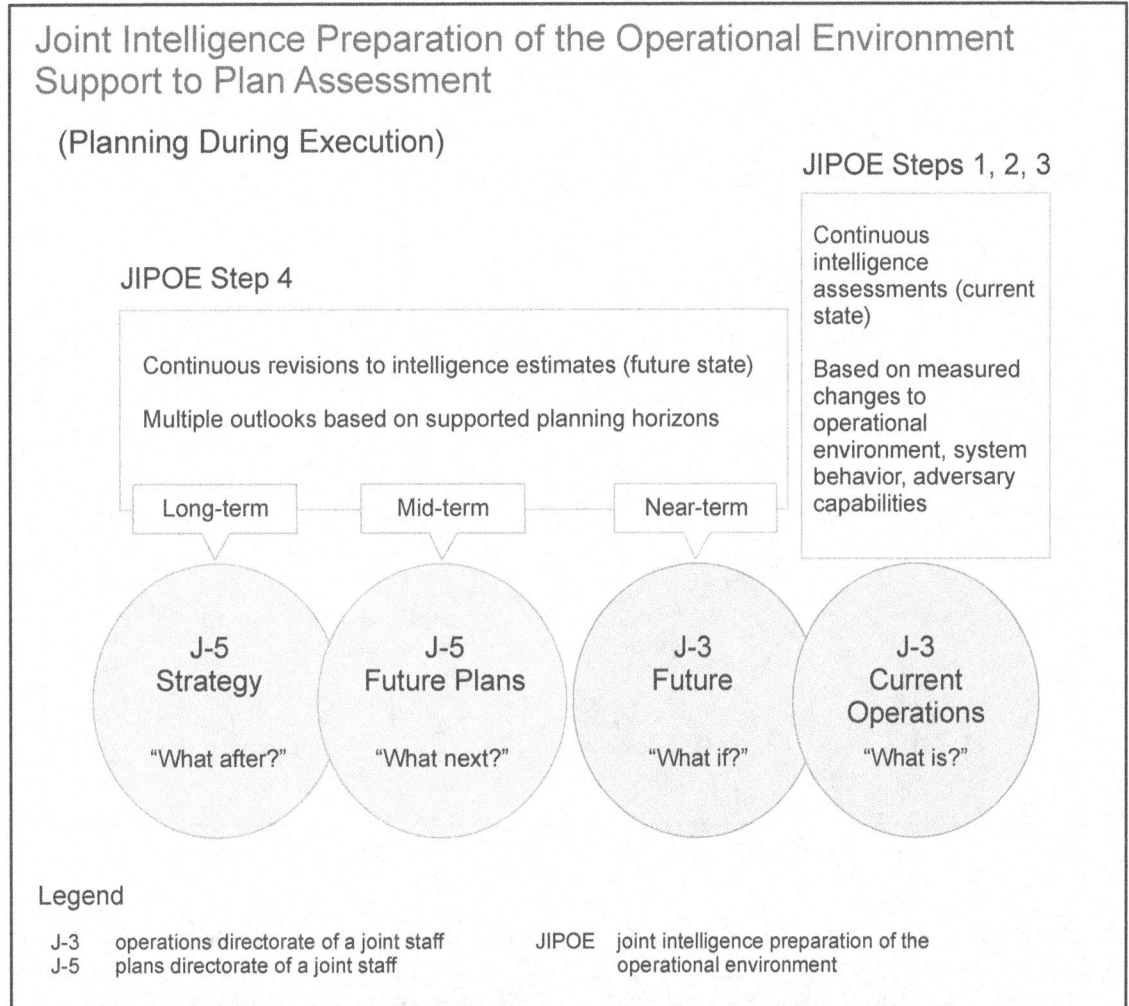

Figure IV-5. Joint Intelligence Preparation of the Operational Environment Support to Plan Assessment

9. Intelligence Support to Strategic and Operational-Level Assessment

Strategic and operational-level assessment efforts concentrate on broad tasks, effects, objectives, and progress toward specified end states (Figure IV-6). Continuous assessment helps the JFC and joint force component commanders determine if the joint force is "doing the right things" to achieve objectives, not just "doing things right." The use of a red team to critically examine the MOE from the perspective of the adversary will help the JFC in measuring the correct information. The JFC can use MOEs to determine progress toward success in those operations for which tactical-level combat assessment ways, means, and measures do not apply.

a. A systems-oriented JIPOE effort is crucial to the identification of adversary COGs, key nodes and links. A COG can be viewed as a source of power that provides moral or physical strength, freedom of action, or will to act. COG analysis requires knowledge of an adversary's physical and psychological strengths and weaknesses and how the adversary organizes, fights, and makes decisions. Human factors analysis of the adversary's leadership

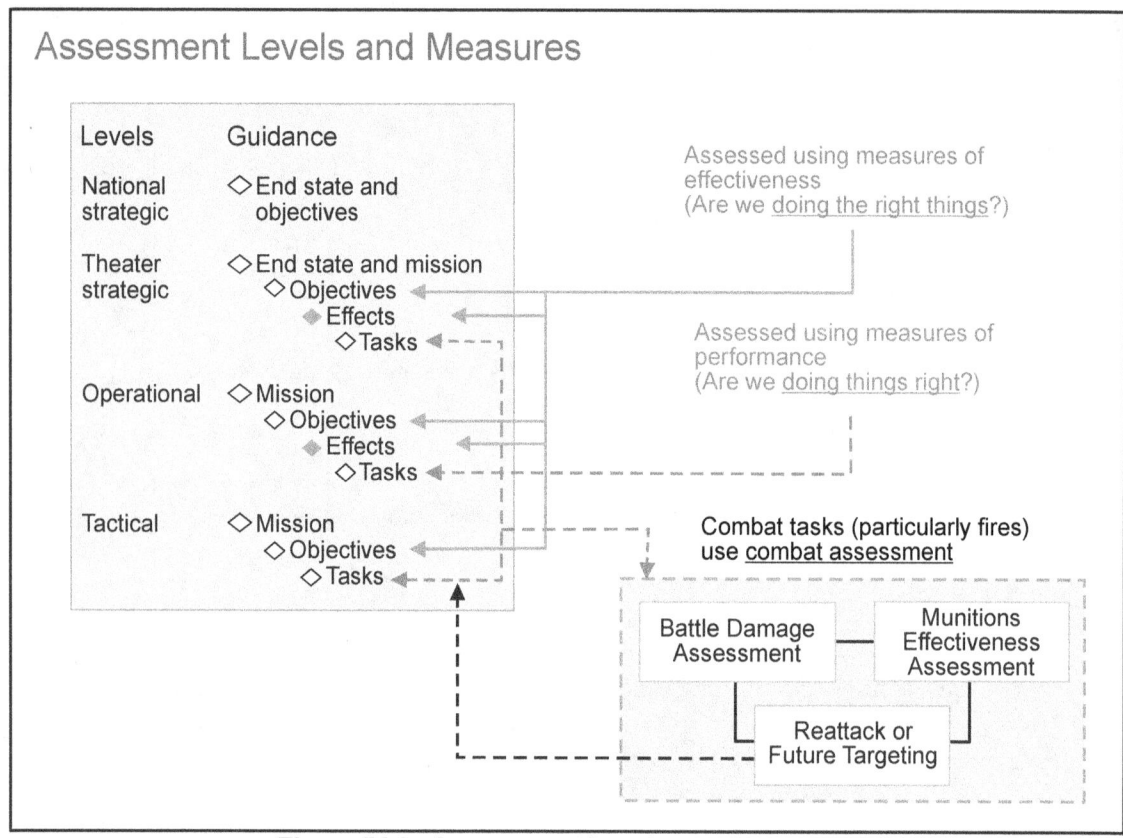

Figure IV-6. Assessment Levels and Measures

characterizes the assessment with strengths, weaknesses, and how decisions are made. Analysts should evaluate biometric, biographic, forensic, and DOMEX data in concert with the JIPOE. The JIPOE analyst must also have a detailed understanding of how each aspect of the OE links to the others and how various permutations of such links and nodes may combine to form COGs. For example, Figure IV-7 shows strategic and operational COGs, each consisting of a set of nodes and links. The operational COG resides in the military system, while the strategic COG focuses in the political system but overlaps with the operational COG.

For additional information on COGs, see JP 5-0, Joint Operation Planning.

   b. JIPOE analysts should assess the importance and vulnerabilities of all operationally relevant nodes and all primary and alternative links to those nodes. This is accomplished by combining an analysis of the constraints imposed by the OE with an evaluation of the adversary's preferred method or means of conducting a specific type of operation or activity (e.g., attack, defense, proliferation, WMD production, financing terrorist cells). The resulting product may take the form of a situation template or model that identifies all the nodes and links associated with individual COAs or options available to the adversary within a specific category of activity. The situation templates may be combined, modeled, and compared to identify key nodes and primary and alternate links among nodes. The consolidated template (event template) provides the means for determining specific events in time and space that if detected would indicate changes in adversary behavior, systems, or the

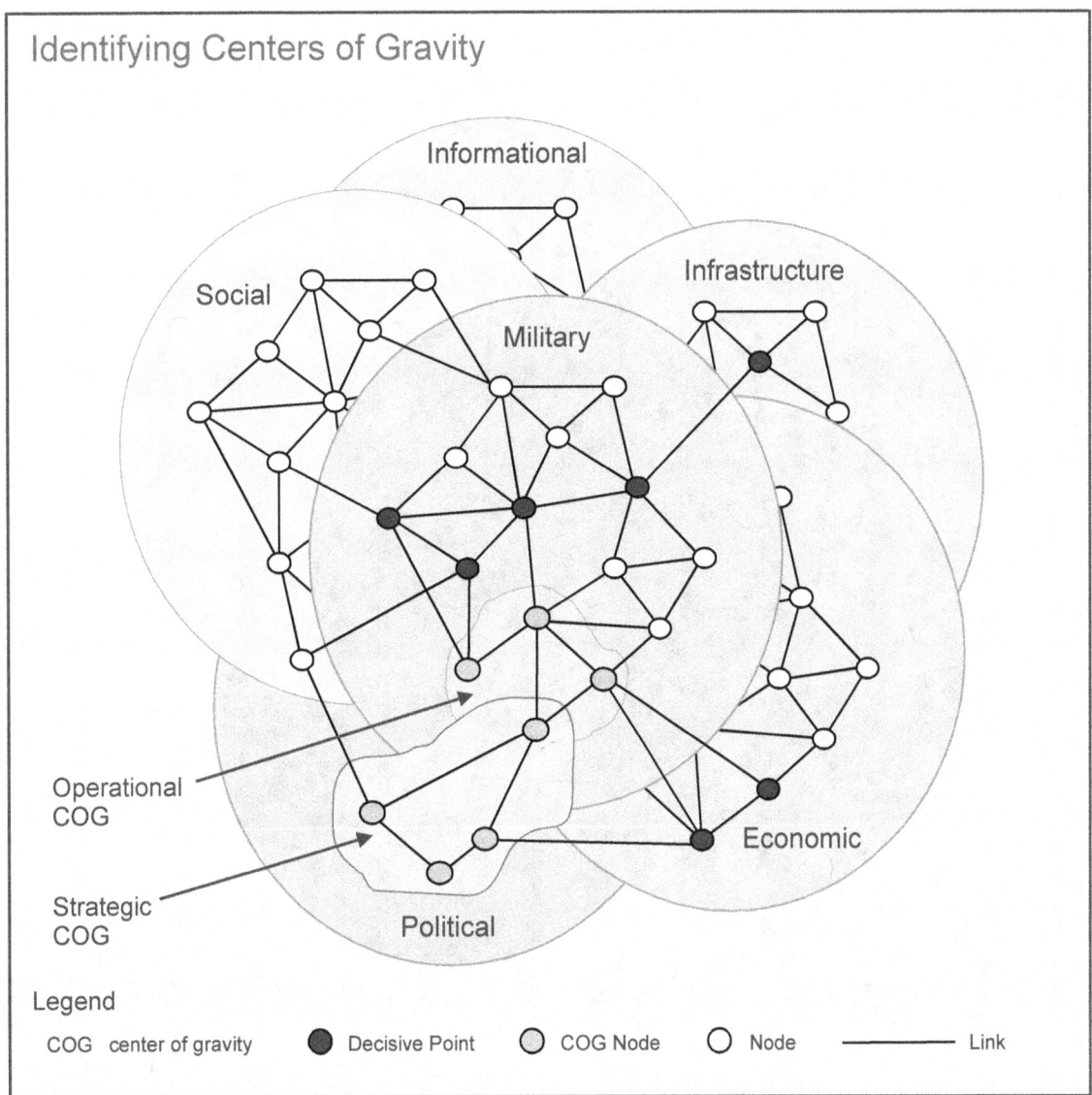

Figure IV-7. Identifying Centers of Gravity

OE. These events, or indicators of change, may be assigned qualitative or quantitative thresholds and may be used as the basis for MOEs. Figure IV-8 is an example of a systems-oriented JIPOE event template demonstrating nodal and link analysis to identify potential indicators of change.

The JIPOE process and its relationship to assessment is described in greater detail in JP 2-01.3, Joint Intelligence Preparation of the Operational Environment.

10. Tactical-Level Assessment

Tactical-level assessment typically uses MOPs to evaluate task accomplishment. The results of tactical tasks are often physical in nature, but also can reflect the impact on specific functions and systems. Tactical-level assessment may include assessing progress by phase lines; neutralization of enemy forces; control of key terrain, people, or resources; and

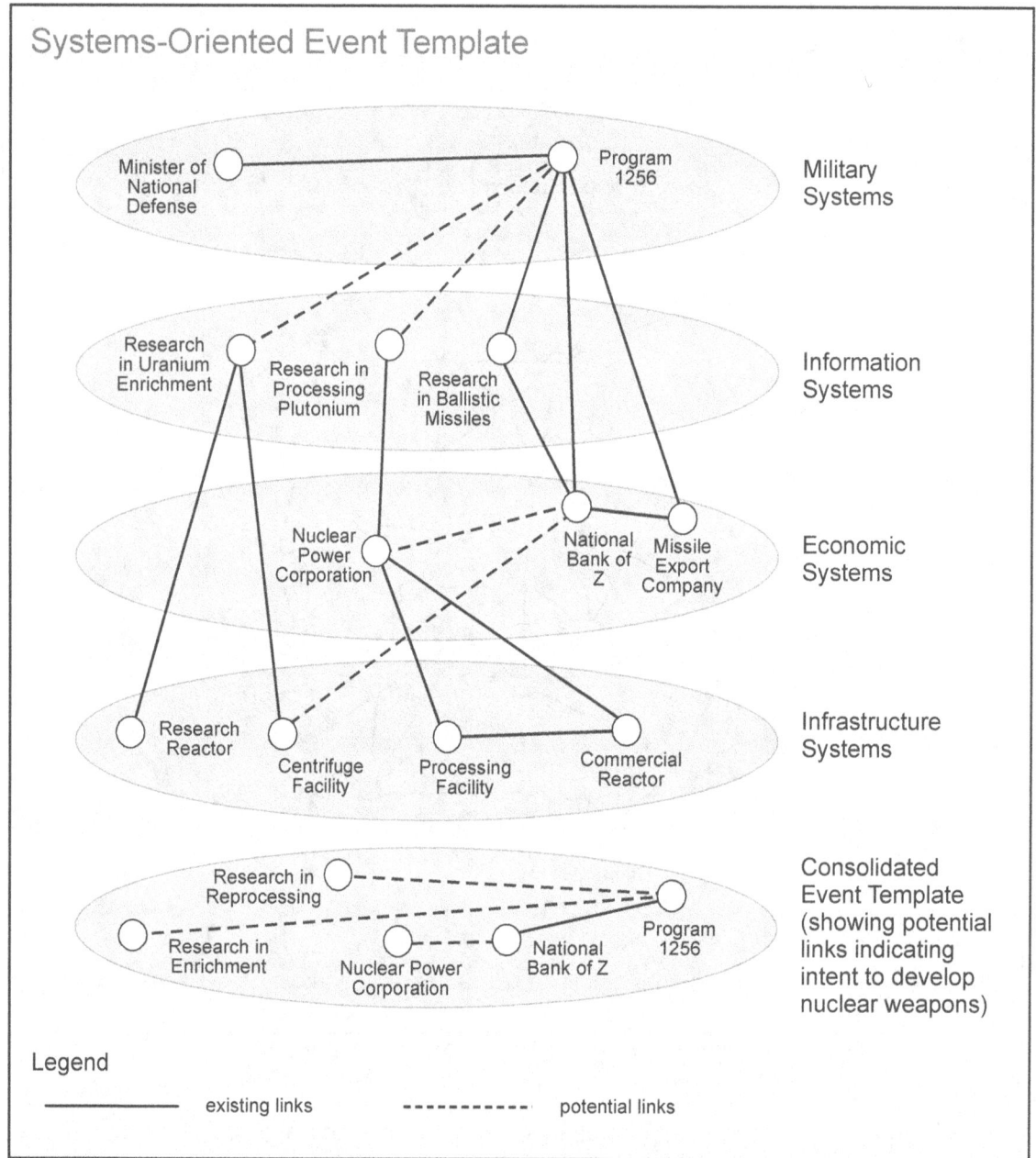

Figure IV-8. Systems-Oriented Event Template

security or reconstruction tasks. Combat assessment is an example of a tactical-level assessment and is a term that can encompass many tactical-level assessment actions. Combat assessment typically focuses on determining the results of weapons engagement (with both lethal and nonlethal capabilities), and is an important component of joint fires and the joint targeting process. It helps the CCDR, the subordinate JFC, and component commanders understand how the joint operation is progressing and assists in shaping future operations. Combat assessments consist of a BDA, munitions effectiveness assessment (MEA), and reattack recommendation.

a. **BDA.** BDA should be a timely and accurate estimate of damage or degradation resulting from the application of military force, lethal or nonlethal, against a target. BDA is primarily an intelligence responsibility with required inputs and coordination from operations and can be federated throughout the IC. The purpose of BDA is to determine the effects of target engagement at the target element level, target level, and target system level in order to support reattack recommendations and development of follow-on targets. The most critical ingredient for effective BDA is a comprehensive understanding of the JFC's objectives and how they relate to a specific target. For BDA to be meaningful, the JFC's objectives and the supporting MOEs must be observable, measurable, and obtainable. The JFC should provide a comprehensive plan, together with an intelligence architecture, to support BDA. This plan must synchronize ISR resources and reporting to effectively/efficiently support timely BDA. Preconflict planning requires collection managers with a thorough understanding of collection systems capabilities (both organic and national) as well as their availability. BDA consists of a physical damage/change assessment phase, functional damage assessment phase, and target system assessment phase.

(1) **Phase I—Physical Damage/Change Assessment.** A physical damage assessment is an estimate of the quantitative extent of physical damage (through munitions blast, fragmentation, and/or fire damage) to a target element based on observed or interpreted damage. Change assessment is the estimate of measurable change to the target resulting from weapons that do not create physical damage. This post-attack target analysis should be a coordinated effort among combat units-supporting organizations. The Joint Staff Targeting and BDA Cell, with J-2 as lead, serves as the national level BDA cell and coordinates CCMD BDA requirements with the IC. Some representative sources for data necessary to make a physical damage assessment include the air tasking order or master air attack plan, mission reports, aircraft cockpit video, weapon system video, visual/verbal reports from ground spotters or combat troops, controllers and observers, artillery target surveillance reports, SIGINT, HUMINT, GEOINT, MASINT, and OSINT. Phase I BDA reporting contains an initial physical damage assessment of hit or miss based usually upon single source data. When appropriate, a reattack recommendation is also included.

(2) **Phase II—Functional Damage/Change Assessment.** The functional damage assessment is an estimate of the effect of military force to degrade or destroy the functional/operational capability of a target to perform its intended mission. Functional assessments are inferred from the assessed physical damage/change and all-source intelligence information. This assessment must include an estimation of the time required for recuperation or replacement of the target's function. BDA analysts compare the original objective for the attack with the current status of the target to determine if the objective was met. Phase II BDA reporting builds upon the phase I initial report and is a fused, all-source product addressing a more detailed description of physical damage, an assessment of the functional damage, inputs to functional assessment of the higher-level target system (phase III), and any applicable MEA comments. When appropriate, a reattack recommendation is also included.

(3) **Phase III—Functional Assessment of the Higher-Level Target System**

(a) Functional assessment of the higher-level target system is a broad assessment of the overall impact on an adversary target system relative to the targeting objectives established. These assessments may be conducted at the CCMD or national-level by fusing all phases I and II BDA reporting on targets within a target system.

(b) BDA phase III produces a target system assessment for the theater of operations. SMEs compile the functional damage assessments of the individual targets within a system and apply it to the current system analysis or enemy order of battle. Although different weapons are involved, the process described above applies to BDA of targets attacked with nonlethal fires as well. SIGINT will often be the most capable collection asset of determining the actual functional damage to the target in these cases.

b. **MEA.** MEA is an assessment of the military force applied in terms of the weapon system and munitions effectiveness to determine and recommend any required changes to the methodology, tactics, weapon systems, munitions, fusing, and/or delivery parameters to increase force effectiveness. MEA is conducted concurrently and interactively with BDA assessments. MEA is primarily the responsibility of component operations, with inputs and coordination from the IC. MEA targeting personnel seek to identify, through a systematic trend analysis, any deficiencies in weapon system and munitions performance or combat tactics by answering the question, "Did the systems (i.e., bomb or jamming) employed perform as expected?" Using a variety of intelligence and operations inputs, to include phase II functional damage assessments, operators prepare a report assessing munitions performance and tactical applications. The report details weapon performance against specified target types. This information could have a crucial impact on future operations and the quality of future BDA. MEA can continue years after the conflict using archived data and information collected by on-site inspections of targets struck during the conflict.

c. **Future Targeting and Reattack Recommendations.** BDA and MEA provide systematic advice on reattacking targets. This culminates in a reattack recommendation and guides further target development. Recommendations range from attacking different targets to changing munitions and/or delivery tactics. The reattack recommendations and future targeting is a combined operations and intelligence function. The reattack recommendation considers if the desired effect was created. That effect is reassessed against its relative importance in the targeting effort, considering if the target is damaged, will it remain inoperable, or when will it be repaired. BDA applies equally to cyberspace operations.

For further information on combat assessment, see JP 3-60, Joint Targeting.

SECTION E. INTELLIGENCE SUPPORT TO EXECUTION BY PHASE

11. General

Intelligence support is crucial to all aspects of execution. For example, CI support to force protection and OPSEC is important during mobilization and deployment; intelligence assessments generated through JIPOE regarding the current status of foreign transportation infrastructure (airfields, seaports, etc.) are vital to the success of deployment and redeployment operations; MEDINT enables decision makers to devise protection measures to mitigate combat-related battle injuries and disease and nonbattle injuries during deployment, employment, and redeployment; and intelligence analyses of threats to air, land, and sea lines of communications are critical to sustainment operations. Immediate, precise, and persistent intelligence support to force employment is a particularly important prerequisite for military success throughout all phases of a joint operation regardless of how the battle evolves, see Figure IV-9. Intelligence staffs must be familiar with specific phasing arrangements of each command OPLAN because the phasing may differ for specific types of operations. During execution, intelligence must stay at least one step ahead of operations and not only support the current phase of the operation, but also simultaneously lay the informational groundwork required for subsequent phases. Execution of joint operations requires optimizing the use of limited intelligence assets and maximizing the efficiency of intelligence production resources and is the ultimate test of the efficacy of intelligence support planning.

12. Intelligence Support During the Shape Phase (Phase 0)

JFCs are able to take actions before committing forces to assist in determining the shape and character of potential future operations. In many cases, these actions enhance bonds between future multinational partners, increase regional understanding, ensure timely access, strengthen future multinational operations, and prevent crises. Intelligence activities

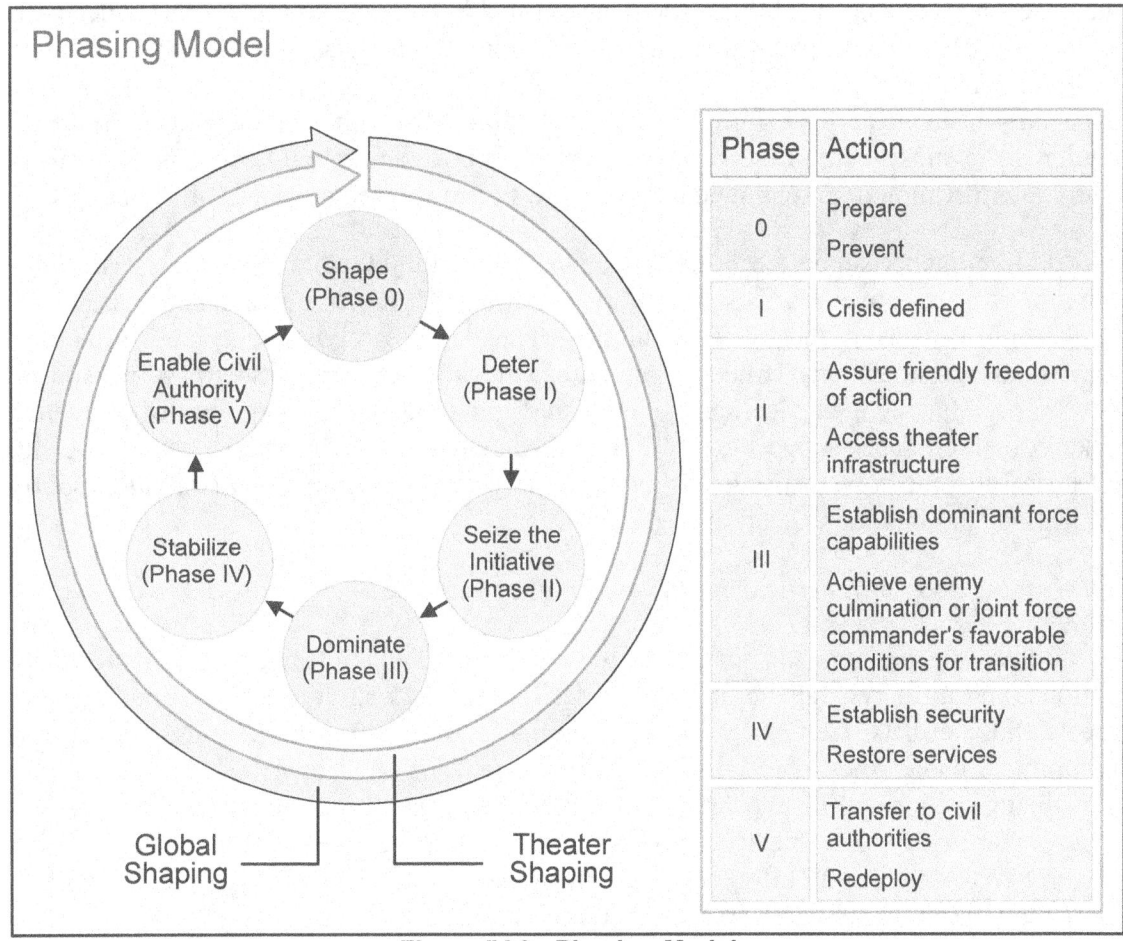

Figure IV-9. Phasing Model

conducted within the context of deliberate planning during the shape phase develop the basics for intelligence operations in subsequent operational phases. Intelligence activities should also be conducted to support phase 0 operations, including those supporting theater campaign plans.

a. Intelligence liaison and the establishment of intelligence sharing arrangements with multinational partners are critical aspects of the shape phase. Whenever possible, and ICW the responsible DNI representative, JFCs should engage PNs by ensuring the participation of US personnel in mutual intelligence training, temporary exchanges of intelligence personnel, federated intelligence arrangements, and the integration and exercise of ISR support architectures. National intelligence cells should be formed as early as possible and a multinational intelligence center established to coordinate their activities. Foreign disclosure procedures should be established and exercised to the maximum extent feasible throughout this phase and PNs participation in the JIPOE effort encouraged.

b. Theater intelligence collection capabilities should be optimized by integrating the various intelligence capabilities of the CCMD and its PNs. Many potential multinational partners have capabilities that may prove invaluable to successful intelligence operations.

c. Information operations intelligence integration (IOII) activities are critical during the shape phase and rely heavily on accurate intelligence. Analysis and assessment of the adversary's leadership capabilities and decision-making process should be performed early to identify effective deterrent messages and actions. Units tasked with identifying host nation audiences should assess messaging potential during all phases of operations, especially influence efforts during phase 0. Additionally, units should identify potential audiences in subsequent phases while still in phase 0 to facilitate IO coordinating efforts. Early identification of potential audiences allows greater responsiveness of IRCs.

d. Intelligence support, especially human sociocultural factors analysis, is essential to maximize the effectiveness of civil-military operations (CMO). An analysis and assessment of the civil dimension in targeted countries, that identifies civil society key influences, individuals, organizations, structures, and areas must be performed as early as possible to determine what civil engagement actions may serve as effective points of influence. Likewise, intelligence support to CMO should be assessed as early as possible to focus the CMO effort and provide the lead-time necessary to provide timely planning, resource allocation, and mission execution.

13. Intelligence Support During the Deter Phase (Phase 1)

Before the initiation of hostilities, the JFC must gain a clear understanding of the national and military strategic objectives; desired and undesired effects; actions likely to create those effects; COGs and decisive points; and required joint, multinational, and nonmilitary capabilities matched to available forces. The joint force J-2 assists the JFC in visualizing and integrating relevant considerations regarding the OE into a plan that will lead to achievement of the objectives and accomplishment of the mission. It is therefore imperative that the JIPOE effort (initiated during the shape phase) provide the JFC with an understanding of the OE at the outset of the deter phase.

a. IOII is also critical during the deter phase. The adversary structure and leadership decision-making process should be continuously monitored and assessed to determine what influence activities may serve as effective deterrents. The receptivity of foreign target audiences to specific messages and actions should also be continuously assessed to support overall influence efforts.

b. During the deter phase, the ongoing JIPOE effort is accelerated to focus on monitoring the current situation while simultaneously assessing adversary capabilities to affect subsequent phases of the operation. JIPOE analysts support early warning by looking for specific indications of imminent adversary activity that may require an immediate response or an acceleration of friendly decision-making processes. JIPOE efforts also concentrate on confirming adversary COGs and support the continuous refinement of estimates of adversary capabilities, dispositions, intentions, and probable COAs within the context of the current situation. At the same time however, JIPOE analysts must look ahead and prepare threat assessments to support future operations planned for the seizing the initiative, dominance, and stabilization phases.

c. During the deter phase, COA development is dependent on detailed TSAs to identify the functional components in the OE that may be affected to support the commander's objectives.

d. GEOINT support is critical during the deter phase. It is essential that any maps, charts, imagery products, and support data to include datum coordinate systems, target material used in a joint operation be coordinated with joint force components, the Joint Staff, OSD, NGA, and PNs. The joint force J-2 works with the JFC staff and component command staffs to identify requirements for updated GEOINT products and submits these requirements through the NGA liaison team.

More detailed guidance regarding GEOINT procedures is contained in JP 2-03, Geospatial Intelligence in Joint Operations.

e. Selected intelligence operations may also serve as a flexible deterrent option—a preplanned, deterrence-oriented action carefully tailored to bring an issue to early resolution without armed conflict. For example, the deployment of additional intelligence resources in the operational area not only increases intelligence collection capabilities and provides early warning, but may also demonstrate US resolve without precipitating an armed response from the adversary. Likewise, intelligence sharing arrangements and exchanges with PNs may reinforce US commitment to the host nation, deterring undesired adversary interactions. Likewise, intelligence sharing arrangements and exchanges with PNs reinforce US commitment to the host nation, deterring undesired adversary interactions

f. Intelligence also supports actions designed to isolate an adversary by identifying their potential allies and sanctuaries. Intelligence may also identify and assess the vulnerability of the adversary's sources of support to interdiction or disruption to include intelligence support from other sources. Neutralizing the adversary's intelligence collection capabilities is particularly important to reinforce their isolation, facilitates their susceptibility to deception operations, and at the same time protects friendly forces from detection.

g. Intelligence support to CMO during the deter phase can amplify operations to isolate the adversary. An analysis and assessment of the civil dimension of potential allies or supporters of the adversary may determine what civil engagement actions may serve as effective points of influence. Additionally, analysis of the civil dimension of friendly countries, especially in countries where US forces will require access for subsequent phases, will suggest appropriate civil engagement targets for CMO that may reduce enemy freedom of action while enhancing that of the US operational commander.

14. Intelligence Support During the Seize the Initiative Phase (Phase II)

As operations commence, the JFC needs to exploit friendly asymmetric advantages and capabilities to shock, demoralize, and disrupt the enemy. The JFC seeks decisive advantage through the use of all available elements of combat power to seize and maintain the initiative, deny the enemy the opportunity to achieve its objectives, and generate in the enemy a mindset of inevitable failure. Additionally, the JFC coordinates with the appropriate interagency representatives through a joint interagency task force, joint interagency coordination group (JIACG), or individually to facilitate coherent use of all instruments of national power in achieving national strategic objectives. JFCs and their J-2s should be on continuous guard against any enemy capability which may impede friendly force deployment from bases, to ports of embarkation, to lodgment areas.

a. The JFC's target intelligence element is more active during this phase compared to previous phases in gathering target nominations, vetting targets, capabilities analysis and target list management all result in a completed joint integrated prioritized target list. During this phase, targeteers monitor ongoing operations recommend changes to the plan, conduct assessment, and provide input for further strategy and planning efforts.

b. IOII and OPSEC are particularly important during this phase. CI supports force protection during deployment from home bases to lodgment areas. I2 supports the identification of key adversary personnel, persons of interest, and their support and facilitation networks. HUMINT, SIGINT, and OSINT sources may detect indications of enemy demoralization and provide insight into the military information support operations success or failure, and potential for exploitation of psychological vulnerabilities. Both the CCMD red team and red cells add value to friendly deception planning efforts. The red team analyzes the proposed plan from the adversary's perspective, and red cells provide insight into the possible times and locations of the adversary's intelligence collection plan. This insight assists deception planners in determining the best times and locations to plant deceptive information designed to mislead adversary intelligence analysts.

JIPOE support to deception planning is discussed in greater detail in JP 2-01.3, Joint Intelligence Preparation of the Operational Environment.

c. Real-time surveillance and dynamic collection management are important throughout the execution of joint operations, but are particularly critical during the seize initiative and the dominate phases. Adversary capabilities must be tracked with a level of persistence and accuracy sufficient to support retargeting and precision engagement. Active, key adversary HUMINT identities should also be discovered, resolved, and tracked as an additional layer for CI and force protection. An integrated collection strategy that fully optimizes the use of all available US, PN, and host-nation collection capabilities assets is essential to persistent surveillance. Furthermore, the CCMD JIOC facilitates collection management through ISR visualization—the continuous real-time monitoring of the status, location, and reporting of intelligence platforms and sensors. ISR visualization provides real-time cross cueing and provides a basis for re-tasking and time-sensitive decision making.

Persistent surveillance and ISR visualization are discussed in greater detail in JP 2-01, Joint and National Intelligence Support to Military Operations.

15. Intelligence Support During the Dominate Phase

During the dominate phase, JFCs conduct sustained combat operations by simultaneously employing conventional, SOF, and information-related capabilities throughout the breadth and depth of the operational area. CMO is executed to preclude civilian interference in attainment of operational objectives or to remove civilians from operational areas. Operations may be linear (i.e., combat power is directed toward the enemy in concert with adjacent units) or nonlinear (i.e., forces orient on objectives without geographic reference to adjacent forces). Some missions and operations (i.e., strategic attack, interdiction, and military information support operations) are executed concurrently with other combat operations to deny the enemy sanctuary, freedom of action, or informational advantage. JFCs may design operations to cause the enemy to concentrate their forces, thereby facilitating their attack by friendly forces, or operations may be designed to prevent the enemy from concentrating their forces, thereby facilitating their isolation and defeat in detail.

a. Intelligence must be equally prepared to support linear and nonlinear operations. Nonlinear operations are particularly challenging due to their emphasis on simultaneous operations along multiple lines of operations. The complexity of nonlinear operations places a premium on a continuous flow of accurate and timely intelligence to help protect individual forces. This flow of intelligence supports precise targeting, mobility, and freedom of action and is enabled by persistent surveillance, dynamic ISR management, and a common intelligence picture (the intelligence portion of the COP).

b. Intelligence must not only support operations during the dominate phase, but also anticipate and address the information requirements for the subsequent stabilize phase. For example, intelligence must be prepared to assist the JFC in determining how to fill the power vacuum after the conclusion of sustained combat operations. In order to set the groundwork for stability, security, transition, and reconstruction operations, the JFC will require detailed intelligence regarding the status of key infrastructure, enemy government organizations and personnel, and anticipated humanitarian needs.

16. Intelligence Support During the Stabilize Phase

Stabilization typically begins with significant military involvement to include some combat operations, then moves increasingly toward enabling civil authority as the threat wanes and civil infrastructures are reestablished. As progress is made, military forces

The use of long endurance, unmanned aircraft systems, such as the MQ-1 Predator, greatly facilitates real-time, persistent surveillance.

increase their focus on supporting the efforts of host nation authorities, US Government departments and agencies, IGOs, and/or NGOs.

a. During the stabilize phase, intelligence collection and analysis should transition from supporting combat operations to focus on actual or potential threats to the joint force (e.g., insurgent groups, criminal elements, terrorist cells). Particular attention should be paid to identifying and assessing the leaders of groups posing potential threats to civil authority and reconstruction efforts. Intelligence should also identify critical infrastructure and analyze its vulnerability to disruption by elements hostile to stabilization efforts. Critical infrastructure vulnerability analysis may require coordination and assistance from other organizations.

b. CI support to force protection is critical during the stabilization phase. Host nation authorities, other organizations, IGOs, and NGOs working closely with US forces may pass information (knowingly or unknowingly) to hostile elements that enables them to interfere with stability operations. Likewise, members of the local populace may have access to US bases in order to provide essential services and friendly forces may recruit former regime officials to participate in stabilization efforts. CI elements help screen and vet foreign personnel and investigate instances of compromised sensitive information.

c. Assessment assists the stabilize phase by assessing the relative effectiveness of IRCs and other operations supporting civil authorities and reconstruction efforts. Additionally, DIA's human factors assessments of foreign leadership's susceptibility to influence can assist commanders in determining the best COAs to achieve stability.

17. Intelligence Support During the Enable Civil Authority Phase

This phase is characterized by the establishment of a legitimate civil authority that is enabled to manage the situation without further outside military assistance. In many cases, the US will transfer responsibility for the political and military affairs of the host nation to another authority. The joint operation is normally terminated when the stated military end states have been met and redeployment of the joint force is accomplished.

a. In some situations, intelligence support may remain in place after termination of the joint operation in order to support the civil authority and/or to continue to monitor the situation. As in the deterrence phase, intelligence resources may serve as a valuable tool for demonstrating US resolve and commitment to the host nation. To facilitate this critical role in establishing friendly relations with the new civil authority, intelligence sharing agreements should be promulgated as soon as practicable.

b. Before the operation is terminated, it is important that all intelligence lessons learned are recorded in appropriate databases and are captured in joint doctrine. Likewise, the joint force J-2 should ensure that all JIPOE products, intelligence assessments, collection plans, and J-2X source registries are appropriately archived. This material may prove valuable to operation planning in the event US forces are directed to redeploy to the area.

CHAPTER V
JOINT, INTERAGENCY, AND MULTINATIONAL INTELLIGENCE SHARING AND COOPERATION

> *"One of the most gratifying features of recent work in intelligence, and one that is quite unique in its long history, has been the growing cooperation established between the American intelligence services and their counterparts throughout the Free World which make common cause with us as we face a common peril."*
>
> **Former Director of Central Intelligence (1953-1961) Allen Dulles,**
> ***The Craft of Intelligence*, 1963**

1. An Intelligence Sharing Environment

The success of joint and multinational operations and interorganizational coordination hinges upon timely and accurate information and intelligence sharing. To prevail, the JFC's decision and execution cycles must be consistently faster than the adversary's and be based on better information. Being faster and better requires having unfettered access to the tasking, collection, processing, analysis, and dissemination of information derived from all available sources. Cooperation, collaboration, and coordination are enabled by an intelligence and information environment that integrates joint, multinational, and interagency partners in a collaborative enterprise. This type of collaborative intelligence sharing environment should be capable of generating and moving intelligence, operational information, and orders to users quickly. The architecture supporting this intelligence environment should be dynamic and capable of providing multinational and interagency participants rapid access to appropriate data. The intelligence sharing architecture is configured to provide the baseline data to support commanders at all levels, and should facilitate the IC in supporting the JFC and subordinate components. CCDRs are responsible for the intelligence sharing architecture within their commands. For contingency operations, subordinate JFCs, supported by their joint force J-2s, are responsible for establishing the joint force intelligence architecture required to accomplish the assigned mission.

a. An intelligence sharing architecture is integral to all intelligence operations. From planning and direction through dissemination and integration, the architecture supports intelligence functions through the Department of Defense information networks (DODIN). The DODIN are the globally interconnected information capabilities, and associated processes for collecting, processing, storing, disseminating, and managing information for warfighters, policy makers, and support personnel, including owned and leased communications and computing systems and services.

b. A collaborative intelligence sharing architecture must support the full range of military operations and support the intelligence requirements of decision makers, from the President down through the joint force's tactical commanders. The architecture incorporates the policies, procedures, reporting structures, trained personnel, automated information processing systems, and connectivity to collect, process, and disseminate intelligence. It also provides support to natural or man-made disaster relief efforts that require military support.

2. Principles for Multinational Intelligence Sharing

"It's not a technical issue any more. It's really more about culture and the 'need to share' rather than the 'need to know."

General James Cartwright, United States Marine Corps Commander,
United States Strategic Command
6 April 2005

In most multinational operations, the JFC will be required to share intelligence with foreign military forces and to coordinate receiving intelligence from those forces. Intelligence efforts must be complementary and take into consideration the intelligence system's strengths, limitations, and each nation's unique and valuable capabilities. In some multinational operations or campaigns, JFCs will be able to use existing international standardization agreements (e.g., North Atlantic Treaty Organization [NATO]) as a basis for establishing rules and policies for conducting joint intelligence operations. Since each multinational operation will be unique, such agreements may have to be modified or amended based on the situation. A JFC participating in a multinational force develops the information sharing policy and procedures for that particular operation based on CCDR guidance and national policy as contained in the *National Policy and Procedures for the Disclosure of Classified Military Information to Foreign Governments and International Organizations (short title: National Disclosure Policy [NDP]-1).* NDP-1 provides policy and procedures in the form of specific disclosure criteria and limitations, definition of terms, release arrangements, and other guidance. The following general principles (see Figure V-1) provide a starting point for creating the necessary policy and procedures:

a. **Align with NDP.** CCMDs and the JFC's foreign disclosure officers (FDOs) require authority before they share classified military information or national intelligence with a foreign entity. Classified military information, as defined in National Security Decision Memorandum 119, *Disclosure of Classified US Military Information to Foreign Governments and International Organizations,* is that set of information which is under the control or jurisdiction of the DOD, its departments or agencies, or is of primary interest to them.

b. **Maintain Unity of Effort.** Intelligence personnel of each nation need to view the threat from multinational as well as national perspectives. A threat to one element of the multinational force by the common adversary must be considered a threat to all multinational force elements. Success in intelligence sharing requires establishing a trusted partnership with foreign counterparts to counter a common threat and maintain a unity of effort.

c. **Make Adjustments.** There will be differences in intelligence doctrine and procedures among the multinational partners. A key to effective multinational intelligence is readiness, beginning with the highest levels of command, to make the adjustments required to resolve significant differences. Major differences may include how intelligence is provided to the commander (jointly or through individual Services or agencies), procedures for sharing information among intelligence agencies, and the degree of security afforded by different communications systems and procedures. Administrative differences that need to

Principles for Multinational Intelligence Sharing

- Align with national disclosure policy.
- Maintain unity of effort.
- Make adjustments.
- Plan early and plan concurrently.
- Share all necessary information.
- Conduct complementary operations.

Figure V-1. Principles for Multinational Intelligence Sharing

be addressed may include classification levels, personnel security clearance standards, requirements for access to sensitive intelligence, and translation requirements.

d. **Plan Early and Plan Concurrently.** JFCs determine what intelligence may be shared with the forces of other nations early in the planning process. NATO and the United States-Republic of Korea Combined Forces Command have developed and exercised intelligence policies and procedures that provide examples of how multinational planning can be done in advance.

e. **Share Necessary Information.** The joint force should share relevant intelligence about the situation and adversary with its multinational partners consistent with respective NDP and JFC guidance. However, information about intelligence sources and methods should not be shared among allies and PNs until approved by the appropriate national-level agency.

(1) In order to share critical intelligence information with allies and PNs efficiently, US intelligence information should be written for release at the most appropriate classification level and given the fewest possible dissemination restrictions within foreign disclosure guidelines. When information relating to a particular source cannot be shared, the intelligence derived from that source may still be provided to other PNs, so long as the information itself does not compromise the source. The J-2 must establish procedures for separating intelligence from sources and methods. Intelligence production agencies often use a "tear line" in classified reports to separate compartmented information from intelligence that can be widely disseminated (the J-2 and component intelligence staff officers keep information above the tear line and disseminate the intelligence below). Having intelligence production agencies use such tear lines will greatly facilitate intelligence sharing.

(2) The joint force J-2 must obtain the necessary foreign disclosure authorization from DIA as soon as possible. J-2 personnel must be knowledgeable of the specific foreign disclosure policy, procedures, and regulations for the operation. The efficient flow of intelligence will be enhanced by the assignment of personnel training in foreign disclosure.

(3) Intelligence support is critical to the commander's inherent force protection mission. Every effort must be made to share data that could impact the commander's force protection mission.

f. **Conduct Complementary Operations.** Intelligence efforts of each nation must be complementary. Each nation will have intelligence system strengths and limitations as well as unique and valuable capabilities. Host-nation security services' capabilities, for example, may contribute significantly to force protection. Furthermore, planning with friendly nations to fill shortfalls, especially linguist requirements, may help overcome such limitations. All intelligence resources and capabilities should be made available for application to the whole of the intelligence problem. Establishing a multinational collection management element is essential for planning and coordinating multinational collection operations.

Additional guidance on intelligence operations in multinational operations can be found in JP 2-01, Joint and National Intelligence Support to Military Operations. *Information on principles and constructs to support multinational operations can be found in JP 3-0,* Joint Operations, *and JP 3-16,* Multinational Operations.

3. Principles for Interorganizational Intelligence Collaboration

Interagency intelligence collaboration should be encouraged whenever possible consistent with applicable national, agency, or organizational procedures and classification guidelines. Successful interagency intelligence collaboration depends on many factors, to include: strong relationship networks, trust and respect among colleagues, sharing a common vision, minimizing territorial issues, continuous communication, and eliminating impediments (see Figure V-2). Liaison personnel are instrumental in bridging gaps and working through barriers that may arise between organizations. An aggressive liaison effort is critical to developing and maintaining unity of effort from initial planning through the execution of operations. However, analysts must base their collaboration on classification, need-to-know, responsibility to share, and applicable national, agency, or organizational guidelines.

a. **Establish Strong Relationship Networks.** Collaboration is built upon the relationships and networks of colleagues that analysts develop throughout their careers. Without knowledge of who one's counterparts are in other intelligence organizations, collaboration on intelligence problems is nearly impossible. Techniques for building relationship networks include attending or hosting conferences, visiting counterparts in other organizations, and exchanges of personnel through interorganizational rotational assignments.

b. **Build Mutual Trust and Respect for Colleagues.** As analysts work intelligence problems, they count on one another to share all relevant data from within their particular field of expertise. For example, imagery analysts should expect SIGINT analysts to provide all relevant information for a particular intelligence problem that they are working and vice versa. Trust and respect is facilitated by proactively communicating information to colleagues and counterparts and by ensuring they are recognized by their organizations for their expertise and contributions.

Principles for Interorganizational Intelligence Collaboration

- Establish strong relationship networks.
- Build mutual trust and respect for colleagues.
- Share a common vision.
- Minimize territorial issues.
- Establish continuous communication.
- Eliminate impediments.

Figure V-2. Principles for Interorganizational Intelligence Collaboration

c. **Share a Common Vision.** A shared common vision should include the goal of providing the most comprehensive, accurate product possible to the customer. Individuals who develop or follow a personal agenda at the expense of other collaborators will, over time, be excluded from the collaborating group. Sharing a common goal among collaborators is facilitated by taking the initiative to alert others when new information becomes available, working together instead of competing, and providing tip-offs of possible collection opportunities. By synchronizing efforts, the strengths of each organization can be maximized for the benefit of all collaborators.

d. **Minimize Territorial Issues.** Reducing the potential for interorganizational conflicts is vital to successful intelligence collaboration. It is important that collaborating analysts recognize that organizational interests are likely to influence the situation and should not be ignored. These issues may be minimized by anticipating their occurrence, developing a plan for addressing them as they emerge, and stressing the mutually beneficial aspects of collaboration such as sharing organizational credit for the final product.

e. **Establish Continuous Communication.** Continuous communication among intelligence colleagues and counterparts is critical to overcoming barriers to collaboration. Formalizing communications mechanisms creates habits and venues of trust. Communication may be enhanced through frequent meetings, teleconferences, phone calls, mail, and e-mail, as well as less formal methods such as periodic working lunches.

f. **Eliminate Impediments.** The leadership of organizations involved in the collaborative enterprise should demonstrate their commitment by taking prompt and decisive action to eliminate any impediments to collaboration. Organizations should implement procedures to incentivize cooperative behavior and consequences to dissuade uncooperative behavior.

4. **Requirements and Standards for an Intelligence Sharing Architecture**

a. **Requirements.** The intelligence sharing architecture must be capable of being tailored to support a specific JFC's information requirements. Intelligence must be provided in a form that is readily understood and directly usable by the recipient without providing the user irrelevant data.

(1) An effective intelligence sharing architecture requires a "reachback" capability—a means by which deployed military forces rapidly access information from, receive support from, and conduct collaboration and information sharing with other units (deployed in theater and from outside the theater). Dissemination of intelligence consists of both "push" and "pull" control principles. The "push" construct allows the higher echelons to push intelligence down to satisfy existing lower echelon requirements or to relay other relevant information to the lower level. The "pull" construct involves direct electronic access to databases, intelligence files, or other repositories by intelligence organizations at all levels. "Push" updates must be based on the JFC's PIRs and other intelligence requirements to ensure that the JFC receives critical information and intelligence. Higher echelons should be aware of PIRs at lower echelons and push PIR related intelligence rather than requiring lower echelons to pull the intelligence. Other information must be available on an as needed "pull" basis so that the joint force J-2 avoids information overload. From SecDef through the tactical commanders, the architecture must provide complete, tailored, all-source intelligence to the decision maker.

"Push" and "pull" control principles are discussed in detail in JP 2-01, Joint and National Intelligence Support to Military Operations.

(2) The intelligence sharing architecture should be constructed so there is no single point of failure. At the same time, the architecture must identify and eliminate any unnecessary duplication of intelligence capabilities so that scarce resources can be focused to meet prioritized requirements.

(3) The intelligence sharing architecture must accommodate the widest possible range of missions and operational scenarios. It must respond to the JFC's requirements for information at any time and any place and support multinational operations with no loss in timeliness. The intelligence operational architecture must incorporate the capabilities of the national and Service intelligence organizations, and provide to the JTF and its components the capability to access national and Service capabilities when necessary.

(4) The intelligence sharing architecture must achieve a seamless integration of the JFC's decision-making and execution cycles with the intelligence process. In developing the operational architecture, the IC should streamline the intelligence process to ensure responsiveness to the JFC's requirements.

(5) The intelligence sharing architecture must be developed so that users can train and exercise with intelligence capabilities in peacetime. Intelligence systems, policies, procedures, connectivity, security, and fusion requirements must be part of joint training exercises and incorporated into simulations. During exercises, capabilities must function exactly as in a real operation, so that the users train in a realistic, seamless environment. The architecture must be configured so that real world databases are preserved and cannot be accidentally or maliciously altered during an exercise.

(6) The intelligence architecture should provide for integration with existing and projected secure teleconferencing and other collaborative communication capabilities. Secure teleconferencing will permit groups of dispersed users to collaborate during the planning and execution of intelligence operations and to coordinate with operational users. Dispersed users include, but are not limited to, JFCs and their subordinate commanders, and theater JIOCs, JISEs, the multinational intelligence centers and/or appropriate multinational partners, the Joint Staff, Services, CSAs, US Government departments and agencies, and national decision makers.

b. **Standards.** The intelligence sharing architecture must meet established standards for survivability, interoperability, security, and compatibility.

(1) **Survivability.** The system design specified in the technical architecture must be as survivable as the command structure it supports. Assets that are vulnerable to damage or destruction must have alternative means of providing required data with minimal risk.

(2) **Interoperability.** It is imperative that intelligence and operations systems architectures be fully interoperable in order to facilitate a COP. The systems architecture should comply with DOD joint net-centric standards and whenever possible, interoperable with PNs systems. The technical architecture should be designed to accommodate interoperability and integration with existing and projected intelligence information systems and with those joint systems that must exchange information with the intelligence technical architecture.

(3) **Security.** Information must be protected in accordance with mandatory security policies. The architecture must be designed so that the widest possible access is permitted without compromising security.

(4) **Compatibility.** The architecture must use common data formats when reengineering existing systems or applications and developing new systems. As a mid-term objective, all components' intelligence systems must be capable of exchanging data, information and intelligence products to allow all-source analysis and fusion. This capability to share data and information must extend to applications, databases, and communications protocols to ensure that intelligence information is compatible with work stations, file servers, and communications links. Both anticipated and unanticipated authorized users must have access to the discoverable, understandable information required to adapt to situations more quickly than the enemy.

c. **Responsibilities.** ICW the Joint Staff, national intelligence agencies, OSD, Defense Information Systems Agency, and Service intelligence organizations, DIA is responsible for implementing, managing, and ensuring compliance with the configuration of information, data, and communications standards for DOD intelligence systems. DIA establishes defense-wide intelligence priorities for attaining interoperability between the tactical, theater, and national intelligence systems and the respective communications systems at each level.

5. Components of an Intelligence Sharing Architecture

a. Organizational Structures

(1) In multinational operations, the multinational force commander exercises command authority over a military force composed of elements from two or more nations. The President retains command authority over US forces, but may place appropriate forces under the operational control of a foreign commander to achieve specific military objectives. However, any large-scale participation of US forces in a major operation will likely be conducted under US command and operational control or through accepted and stable regional security organizations such as NATO. Therefore, in most multinational operations, the JFC will be required to share intelligence with foreign military forces and to coordinate receiving intelligence from those forces. In some circumstances, the JFC will need to seek authority to go outside the usual political-military channels to provide information to NGOs. Unique intelligence policy and dissemination criteria will have to be tailored to each multinational operation.

(a) A multinational intelligence center is necessary for merging and prioritizing the intelligence requirements from each participating nation and for acquiring and fusing all nations' intelligence contributions. Likewise, the center should coordinate the intelligence collection planning and intelligence and surveillance operations of each nation. The multinational intelligence center should include representatives from all nations participating in the multinational operation. Designating a single director of intelligence for the multinational command will greatly assist in resolving potential disagreements among the multinational members. Figure V-3 depicts a notional multinational intelligence architecture.

(b) Intelligence liaison is critical between commands and among supporting and supported organizations. Liaison personnel are instrumental in resolving problems resulting from language barriers and cultural and operational differences that normally occur in multinational operations. Because of the inherent complexities associated with multinational operations, an aggressive liaison effort is critical to developing and maintaining unity of effort. A robust liaison effort with sufficient communications is particularly critical in the initial stages of planning and forming a coalition, particularly when the US intelligence network is not yet established. US SOF may be assigned down to coalition brigade level to act as coalition liaison elements or support teams. These teams have the ability to receive and disseminate intelligence directly to and from their counterparts. The team members are selected based upon their language and cultural knowledge of the area and are in direct communication with either their combined joint special operations task force, or the next higher special operations command and control element.

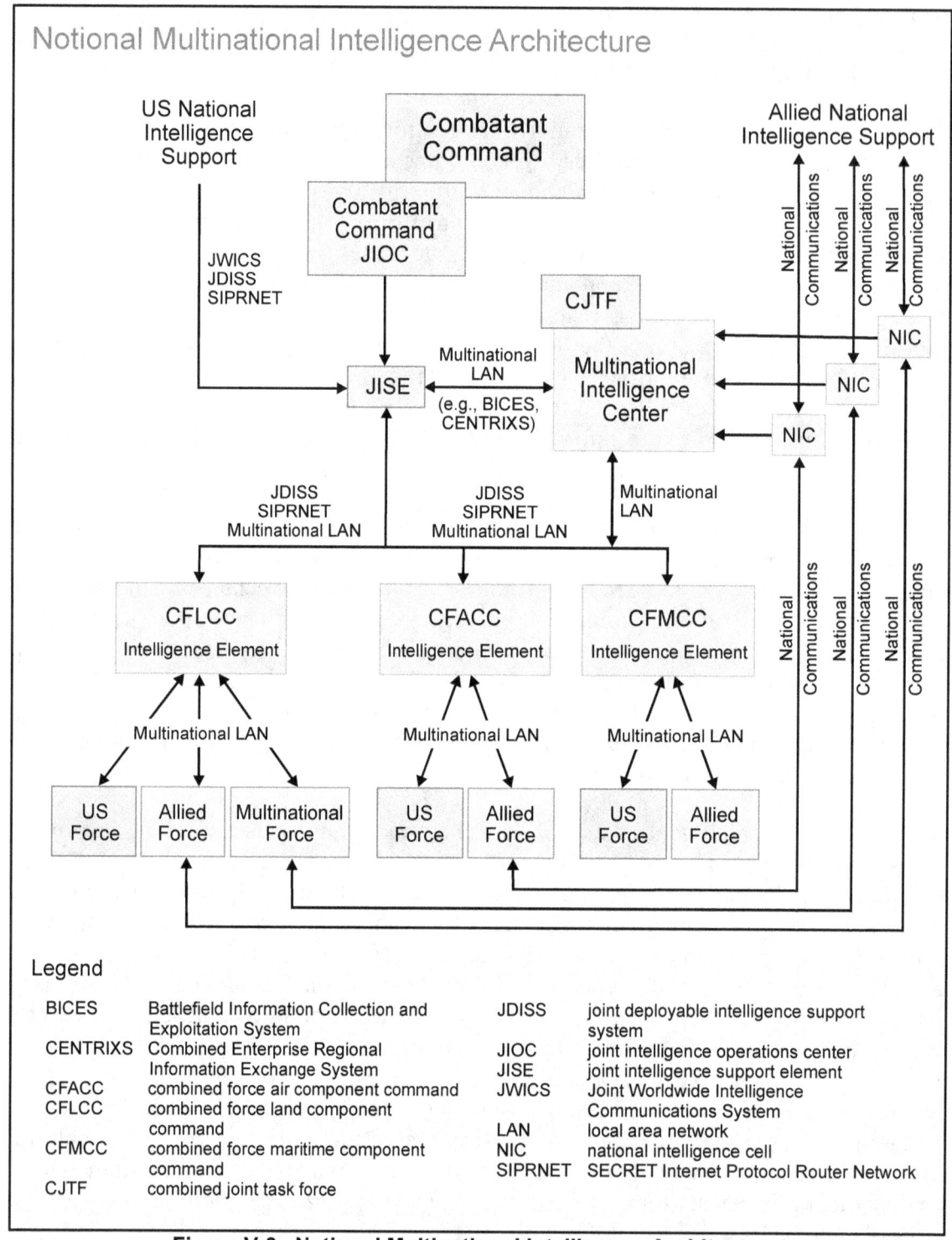

Figure V-3. Notional Multinational Intelligence Architecture

(2) During interagency coordination, information and intelligence sharing are facilitated by each CCMD's JIOC, DNI representative, DIA forward element, and JIACG.

(a) The CCMD JIOC is the theater focal point to plan, synchronize, coordinate, and integrate the full range of intelligence operations in the GCCs' AOR. The JIOC works with the DNI representative to the CCMD and liaison personnel from DOD and non-DOD national intelligence organizations to ensure all relevant intelligence and information is fully shared in the most timely manner possible.

(b) The JIACG facilitates the application of the instruments of national power in a coherent manner and provides a means to integrate interagency perspective into military planning and execution. The JIACG, consisting of various representatives from US Government departments and agencies, serves as a multifunctional advisory element that can facilitate information sharing, operational-level planning and coordination, and political-military synthesis across the interagency community for the CCDR and staff. A typical JIACG may connect to the various US embassies and their country teams as well as to national-level planners. Its primary role is to bridge the gap between civilian agency and military campaign planning efforts for regional engagement and potential regional crises. Specific objectives of the JIACG are to:

1. Improve operational interagency planning and execution.

2. Exercise secure collaboration processes and procedures with participating agencies.

3. Promote continuous relationships among interagency planners.

Further information on the JIACG is contained in JP 3-08, Interorganizational Coordination During Joint Operations.

b. **Systems Network.** A network of integrated work stations, file servers, and communications links comprises the second component of an integrated intelligence architecture. The components of the systems network must work together and comply with the evolving defense information infrastructure, COP, net centric data strategies, and DOD Information Technology Standards Registry, to create the interoperable collaborative information environment required to support joint and multinational operations and interagency coordination. The network includes direct connectivity by appropriate communications or communications relay link (landline, radio, satellite, and others as appropriate) and broadcast capability to support time-sensitive needs.

(1) The DODIN allows data collected by any means to be communicated directly to a user or to a processing site or platform by the most efficient path, then passed on or through to the user as appropriate. A critical aspect of the information network is its ability to make all intelligence accessible by way of standardized file servers to standards-compliant workstations.

(2) The DOD Intelligence Information System enterprise is the global set of resources (people, facilities, hardware, software, and processes) that provide information technology and information management services to the DOD military IC through a tightly integrated, interconnected, and geographically distributed regional service center

architecture. The enterprise capabilities are centrally managed and decentrally executed under the authority and direction of the DIA Chief Information Officer.

(3) To maximize the utility of the systems architecture, systems must be interoperable. Standard communications protocols and standard encryption devices must be available at all echelons. The systems architecture should have the flexibility to accommodate, not replace, existing warning and direct support systems. The systems architecture is intended to be sufficiently agile to allow updating with innovative technology or to overlay additional capabilities using existing communications carriers. Until an effective multilevel security system is in place with joint forces, the intelligence architecture must support three possible levels of information: SCI, non-SCI (TOP SECRET and below), and intelligence releasable to allies and PNs.

(a) **SCI Support.** The Joint Worldwide Intelligence Communications System (JWICS) is a SCI element of the Defense Information System Network. JWICS incorporates advanced networking technologies that permit point-to-point or multipoint information exchange involving voice, text, graphics, data, and video teleconferencing. Additionally, the joint deployable intelligence support system (JDISS) provides a transportable workstation and communications suite that electronically extends a joint intelligence center to a JTF or other tactical user. Both systems currently form the common baseline for all SCI support systems in the intelligence architecture.

<u>1.</u> **JWICS** satisfies the requirement for secure, high-speed, multimedia transmission services for SCI. JWICS incorporates advanced networking technologies that permit greater throughput and capacity, making possible the use of applications that take advantage of multimedia technologies including video teleconferencing. Video-capable JWICS nodes can create, receive, transmit, and store video images as well as voice, text, graphics, and data. Information can be either broadcast or shared interactively among JWICS subscribers on a point-to-point or multipoint basis. The JWICS circuit can be managed by way of allocation of bandwidth, allowing simultaneous use of the link for multiple applications.

<u>2.</u> **JDISS** provides the standard workstation server software configuration. The basic backbone for the dissemination of intelligence to and from deployed JDISS nodes is the JWICS network. Where JWICS is not required or not available, JDISS has a versatile communications capability that can interface with existing communications systems, such as tri-Service tactical communications systems. The system architecture optimizes flexibility to focus intelligence efforts efficiently and ensures that support is maximized for a joint force engaged in military operations.

**COMBINED ENTERPRISE REGIONAL INFORMATION
EXCHANGE SYSTEM**

"US Central Command (USCENTCOM) established a Coalition Intelligence Center...to leverage the access, intelligence expertise and perspectives of our 68 Operation ENDURING FREEDOM coalition partners. Intelligence representatives from traditional Commonwealth and North Atlantic Treaty Organization partners (United Kingdom, Canada, Australia, New Zealand,

Germany, Denmark, France) were integrated into daily operations on a more comprehensive basis; useful terrorism exchange relationships were established with several nontraditional partners resident at USCENTCOM Headquarters, to include Russia, Uzbekistan and Ethiopia. The Combined Enterprise Regional Information Exchange System (CENTRIXS) [was] designed for exactly this type of scenario....CENTRIXS links into Global Command and Control System Common Operation Picture servers and facilitates operations/intelligence sharing at releasable levels through use of multilevel database replication guards, facilitating rapid Coalition access to US databases without human intervention. Coalition partners have given the system high marks and access daily products for local and national decision maker situational awareness....This is a 'big deal' in terms of information superiority—we simply cannot move very far ahead without enforced standards, discipline, and sustained funding emphasis in this regard."

**Brigadier General John F. Kimmons, US Army
Director of Intelligence, USCENTCOM
Testimony to the US House of Representatives
Permanent Select Committee on Intelligence
23 May 2002**

(c) **Multinational Support.** Multinational intelligence sharing should be facilitated by establishing a shared local area network using systems such as the battlefield information collection and exploitation system, the Combined Enterprise Regional Information Exchange System (CENTRIXS), or other emerging multinational mission networks. As the current DOD multinational information-sharing portion of the DODIN, CENTRIXS defines the standards for establishing and maintaining multinational connectivity at the tactical and operational level, with reachback capability to the strategic level. Missions requiring information sharing with NGO partners can leverage the All Partners Access Network which facilitates information sharing between military and non-military organizations. The establishment of a collaborative environment for mission partners will facilitate information sharing within a multinational force. Operations require US forces and mission partners to understand the tactics, techniques, and procedures for establishing and operating a collaborative network that is enabled by the technical capabilities that each PN brings to the operation. Within a collaborative environment with PNs, the US commander needs to balance "need-to-know" with the responsibility to share, and understand the associated risk.

c. Standardized procedures for disseminating and exchanging intelligence constitute the third component of an intelligence sharing architecture. These procedures are critical to joint and multinational operations and interagency coordination.

(1) The procedures and methodology for intelligence and information sharing should be conceived and exercised as part of multinational and interagency planning before operations begin. Special attention should be paid to intelligence classification and levels of access of multinational personnel. To this end, the J-2 should consider adding extra FDO billets to facilitate information sharing. The effectiveness of the procedures and methodology should be monitored and, when necessary, adapted during operations to meet changing circumstances.

EXAMPLES OF MULTINATIONAL INTELLIGENCE SHARING LEVELS

Procedures established to support US and United Nations (UN) forces in Somalia as members of the UN Operations in Somalia (UNOSOM II) effort used two levels of intelligence: Level 1 data could be shown to but not retained by coalition forces or the UN, while Level 2 data was cleared for release to the coalition and the UN. Level 1 intelligence remained within US-only channels, while Level 2 data flowed to the UNOSOM II information center in Mogadishu either from the UN Headquarters or via the US joint intelligence support element.

In some situations there may be more than two levels of intelligence required. For example, an operation involving a mixture of North Atlantic Treaty Organization (NATO) and non-NATO forces could have "US Only," "Releasable to NATO," and "Releasable to Non-NATO" levels. The multinational force commander (MNFC) will play a major role in advising the national intelligence community on the intelligence requirements for each of the allies and coalition partners. The MNFC will need to recommend what intelligence should be provided to each member.

(2) Following established guidelines, data should be passed to standardized data stores as soon as possible. In some situations the data will require processing and exploitation to convert it into a format compatible with certain storage means. However, whenever possible, data not requiring prior conversion should be automatically passed to the standardized data stores without processing. Automated posting of data, combined with flexible connectivity to computer systems at all echelons of the command structure and within the Services, allows intelligence analysts to access imagery and multiple databases while concurrently producing intelligence products in response to specific mission requirements. For example, high-resolution video collected by an unmanned aerial system can be viewed in near-real time at a downlink processing site, but disseminating this video requires high bandwidth. The unprocessed video can be relayed directly by fiber optic line or satellite to a headquarters' element or JTF JISE. At the same time, targeting information can be reported to tactical elements by voice communications or message. Selected video frames can be captured by JDISS and made available to all users over the intelligence architecture. Information processed by a headquarters element or JTF JISE could, in turn, be transmitted or made available by JWICS and/or JDISS. In this example, all the capabilities linked to and by the intelligence sharing architecture are exercised including both "pull" and "push" dissemination. The information is made available for a variety of users' needs and is included in products and reports that serve multiple purposes for the tactical users.

Intentionally Blank

APPENDIX A
INTELLIGENCE CONFIDENCE LEVELS IN ANALYTIC JUDGMENTS

a. Intelligence analysts should distinguish between what is known with confidence based on the facts of the situation and the OE and what are untested assumptions. Intelligence can be facts that have been observed, or it can be a conclusion based on facts of such certainty that it is considered to be knowledge. Intelligence can also be conclusions and estimates deduced from incomplete sets of facts or induced from potentially related facts. The commander's determination of appropriate objectives and operations may rest on knowing whether intelligence is "fact" or "assumption," and knowing the particular logic used to develop an intelligence estimate, as well as knowing the confidence level the J-2 places on the provided intelligence and related analytic conclusions.

b. The following chart (Figure A-1) is intended to illustrate confidence in analytic judgments intelligence personnel may use to indicate a subjective judgment regarding the degree of confidence they place on the analytic conclusions contained in intelligence products. Confidence levels may be used by intelligence producers to present analysis and conclusions to decision makers in a uniform, consistent manner.

Expressing Confidence In Analytic Judgments

Confidence in a judgment is based on three factors: number of key assumptions required, the credibility and diversity of sourcing in the knowledge base, and the strength of argumentation. Each factor should be assessed independently and then in concert with the other factors to determine the confidence level. Multiple judgments in a product may contain varying levels of confidence. Confidence levels are stated as Low, Moderate, and High.

Phrases such as "we judge" or "we assess" are used to call attention to a product's key assessment. Supporting assessments may use likelihood terms or expressions to distinguish them from assumptions or reporting. Below are guidelines for likeliness terms and the confidence levels with which they correspond.

Low	Moderate	High
• Uncorroborated information from good or marginal sources • Many assumptions • Mostly weak logical inferences, minimal methods application • Glaring intelligence gaps exist	• Partially corroborated information from good sources • Several assumptions • Mix of strong and weak inferences and methods • Minimum intelligence gaps exist	• Well-corroborated information from proven sources • Minimal assumptions • Strong logical inferences and methods • No or minor intelligence gaps exist
Terms/Expressions	**Terms/Expressions**	**Terms/Expressions**
• Possible • Could, may, might • Cannot judge, unclear	• Likely, unlikely • Probable, improbable • Anticipate, appear	• Will, will not • Almost certainly, remote • Highly likely, highly unlikely • Expect, assert, affirm

Figure A-1. Expressing Confidence in Analytic Judgments

APPENDIX B
INTELLIGENCE DISCIPLINES

Intelligence disciplines are well-defined areas that involve specific categories, collections, and analysis with emphasis on technical or human resources capabilities (see Figure B-1).

1. Geospatial Intelligence

GEOINT is the exploitation and analysis of imagery and geospatial information to describe, assess, and visually depict physical features and geographically referenced activities on the Earth. GEOINT consists of imagery, IMINT, and geospatial information. GEOINT encompasses a range of products from simple IMINT reports to complex sets of layered foundation and intelligence/mission-specific data. GEOINT products are often developed through a "value added" process, in which both the producer and the user of GEOINT update a database or product with current information. Full motion video is another GEOINT intelligence collection capability that has proven key to activity-based intelligence collection by providing near-continuous or sustained collection on designated targets. The three components of GEOINT (imagery, IMINT, and geospatial information) are discussed below.

a. **Imagery** is a likeness or presentation of any natural or man-made feature or related object or activity and the positional data acquired at the same time the likeness or representation was acquired, including products produced by space-based national intelligence reconnaissance systems, and likenesses or presentations produced by satellites, airborne platforms, unmanned aerial vehicles, or other similar means (this does not include handheld photography). It is used extensively to update GEOINT foundation data and serves as GEOINT's primary source of information when exploited through IMINT. The vast majority of modern imagery products are created, processed, and disseminated in an electronic still or motion format. A few film-based systems still exist to fulfill special requirements.

b. **IMINT** is the technical, geographic, and intelligence information derived through the interpretation or analysis of imagery and collateral materials. It includes exploitation of imagery data derived from electro-optical (EO), radar, infrared (IR), multi-spectral, and laser sensors. These sensors produce images of objects optically, electronically, or digitally on film, electronic display devices, or other media. A wide variety of platforms and sensors support IMINT operations. IMINT is a product that is the result of processing and exploiting raw imagery (information) and creating an analyzed product (intelligence). An image alone is only information in the form of pixels, digits, or other forms of graphic representation and the data behind that portrayal. Imagery source categories include commercial remote sensing, EO, ground photo, hyperspectral imagery (HSI), IR, lidar multispectral imagery (MSI), panchromatic, polarmetric, and synthetic aperture radar.

(1) **EO sensors** provide digital imagery data in the IR, visible, and/or ultraviolet regions of the electromagnetic spectrum. Panchromatic EO sensors detect a broad segment of the visible spectrum, while other EO sensors focus on IR energy or detect multiple narrow bands across the EO spectrum. EO sensors generally provide a high level of detail or

Intelligence Disciplines, Subcategories, Sources, and Applications

GEOINT – Geospatial Intelligence

- Imagery
- IMINT – imagery intelligence
- Geospatial information

HUMINT – Human Intelligence

- Debriefings
- Interrogation operations
- Source operations

SIGINT – Signals Intelligence

- COMINT – communications intelligence
- ELINT – electronic intelligence
  - technical ELINT
  - operational ELINT
- FISINT – foreign instrumentation signals intelligence

MASINT – Measurement and Signature Intelligence

- Electromagnetic data
- Radar data
- Radio frequency data
- Geophysical data
- Materials data
- Nuclear radiation data

OSINT – Open-Source Intelligence

- Academia
- Interagency
- Newspapers/periodicals
- Due diligence
- Media broadcasts
- Internet
- Alternative collections

TECHINT – Technical Intelligence

- Weapon system intelligence
- Scientific intelligence

CI – Counterintelligence

Applications

- Biometrics-enabled intelligence
- Forensics-enabled intelligence
- Document and media exploitation
- Identify intelligence

Figure B-1. Intelligence Disciplines, Subcategories, Sources, and Applications

resolution as compared to radar or other sensors, but cannot successfully through bad weather. Panchromatic sensors provide the highest level of resolution, but cannot image at night. EO offers many advantages over non-digital (i.e., film-based) systems including improved timeliness, greater dissemination options, imagery enhancement, and additional exploitation methods.

(a) **IR imaging sensors** provide a pictorial representation of the contrasts in thermal IR emissions between objects and their surroundings, and are effective during periods of limited visibility such as at night or in inclement weather. A unique capability available with IR sensing is the ability to detect ongoing activity (based on heat levels) as well as past activity through residual thermal effects.

(b) **Spectral imagery sensors** operate in discrete spectral bands, typically in the IR and visible regions of the electromagnetic spectrum. Spectral imagery is useful for characterizing the environment or detecting and locating objects with known material signatures. A multispectral image is made from a set of images taken at different intervals of continuous wavelengths, called "bands," which when viewed together produce a color image. It is similar to using a color filter when taking a black and white picture. Only the rays of the color of the filter are allowed to reach the film. Traditionally, multispectral sensors contain a red, green, and blue band, but can contain tens of bands that image regions of the electromagnetic spectrum to which the human eye is not sensitive. The advantage of taking multispectral images is the ability to discern different materials through their spectral signature. This information can be transferred into intelligence and aid in the analysis of targets. Some **MSI** sensors provide low resolution, large area coverage that may reveal details not apparent in higher resolution panchromatic imagery. Map-like products can be created from MSI data for improved area familiarization and orientation. **HSI** is derived from subdividing the electromagnetic spectrum into very narrow bandwidths which may be combined with, or subtracted from each other in various ways to form images useful in precise terrain or target analysis. For example, HSI can analyze electromagnetic propagation characteristics, detect industrial chemical emissions, identify atmospheric properties, improve detection of blowing sand and dust, and evaluate snow depths.

(2) **Radar imaging sensors** provide all weather imaging capabilities and the primary night capability. Radar imagery is formed from reflected energy in the radio frequency portion of the electromagnetic spectrum. Some radar sensors provide moving target indicator capability to detect and locate moving targets such as armor and other vehicles.

(3) **Lidar sensors** are similar to radar, transmitting laser pulses to a target and recording the time required for the pulses to return to the sensor receiver. Lidar can be used to measure shoreline and beach volume changes, conduct flood risk analysis, identify waterflow issues, and augment transportation mapping applications. Lidar supports large scale production of high-resolution digital elevation products displaying accurate, highly detailed three-dimensional models of structures and terrain invaluable for operational planning and mission rehearsal.

c. **Geospatial information** identifies the geographic location and characteristics of natural or constructed features and boundaries on the Earth, including: statistical data; information derived from, among other things, remote sensing, mapping, and surveying technologies; and mapping, charting, geodetic data, and related products. This information is used for military planning, training, and operations including navigation, mission planning and rehearsal, modeling and simulation, and targeting.

GEOINT is addressed in detail in JP 2-03, Geospatial Intelligence in Joint Operations.

2. Human Intelligence

HUMINT is a category of intelligence derived from information collected and provided by human sources. There are 15 defense HUMINT executors. Collectively, they are known as the Defense HUMINT Enterprise. The Defense HUMINT Enterprise is capable of providing full-spectrum HUMINT support to military operations. The Defense HUMINT Enterprise and its members also partner with multinational HUMINT elements during multinational operations.

For additional information on HUMINT, see JP 2-01.2, Counterintelligence and Human Intelligence in Joint Operations.

a. **Intelligence Interrogation.** Intelligence interrogation is a systematic process of using interrogation approaches to question a captured or detained person to obtain reliable information to satisfy intelligence collection requirements. Trained interrogators with current certification operating under DOD authority are permitted to conduct intelligence interrogations.

For more information on interrogation, see Field Manual 2-22.3, Human Intelligence Collection Operations, *which is the source for procedures on the conduct of intelligence interrogations. For guidance on debriefing and questioning, see Department of Defense Directive (DODD) 3115.09,* DOD Intelligence Interrogations, Detainee Debriefings, and Tactical Questioning.

b. **Source Operations.** Designated and trained personnel in a unit with the "source operations" mission may develop information through the direct and indirect questioning of overt or clandestine sources. These personnel operate under the authority and direction of a designated defense HUMINT executor.

For more information see DODD 5200.37, Management and Execution of Defense Human

> **There are important legal restrictions on interrogation and source operations. Federal law and Department of Defense policy require that these operations be carried out only by trained and certified personnel in a unit with this mission. Violators may be punished under the Uniform Code of Military Justice. See DODD 3115.09, DOD Intelligence Interrogations, Detainee Debriefings, and Tactical Questioning, for more detailed discussion on interrogation.**

Intelligence (HUMINT), *and DOD 5240.1-R,* Procedures Governing the Activities of DOD Intelligence Components that Affect United States Persons.

   (1) **"Walk-in"** sources are unsolicited personnel who volunteer information.

For more information, see Defense HUMINT Enterprise Manual 3300.001, DIA HUMINT Manual, Volume I, Collection Requirements, *and Defense HUMINT Enterprise Manual 3301.002,* DIA HUMINT Manual, Volume II: Collection Operations.

   (2) **Developed sources** that are met over a period of time and provide information based on operational requirements.

   (3) **Unwitting persons,** with access to sensitive information.

   c. **Debriefing.** Debriefing is the process of questioning cooperative human sources to satisfy intelligence requirements, consistent with applicable law. The source usually is not in custody and usually is willing to cooperate. Debriefing may be conducted at all echelons and in all OEs. Through debriefing, face-to-face meetings, conversations, and elicitation, information may be obtained from a variety of human sources, such as:

   (1) **Friendly forces personnel,** who typically include high-risk mission personnel such as combat patrols, aircraft pilots and crew, long range surveillance teams, and SOF, but can include any personnel with information that can be used for intelligence analysis concerning the adversary or other relevant aspects of the OE. Combat intelligence, if reported immediately during an operational mission, can be used to redirect tactical assets to attack enemy forces on a time sensitive basis.

   (2) **Refugees/displaced persons,** particularly if they are from enemy controlled areas of operational interest, or if their former placement or employment gave them access to information of intelligence value.

   (3) **Returnees,** including returned prisoners of war, defectors, freed hostages, and personnel reported as missing in action.

   (4) **Volunteers,** who freely offer information of value to US forces on their own initiative.

HUMINT is addressed in detail in JP 2-01.2, Counterintelligence and Human Intelligence Support to Joint Operations.

3. Signals Intelligence

SIGINT is intelligence produced by exploiting foreign communications systems and noncommunications emitters. SIGINT provides unique intelligence information, complements intelligence derived from other sources and is often used for cueing other sensors to potential targets of interest. For example, SIGINT which identifies activity of interest may be used to cue GEOINT to confirm that activity. Conversely, changes detected by GEOINT can cue SIGINT collection against new targets. The discipline is subdivided into three subcategories: **communications intelligence (COMINT), ELINT, and foreign instrumentation signals intelligence (FISINT).**

    a. **COMINT** is intelligence and technical information derived from collecting and processing intercepted foreign communications passed by radio, wire, or other electromagnetic means. COMINT also may include imagery, when pictures or diagrams are encoded by a computer network/radio frequency method for storage and/or transmission. The imagery can be static or streaming.

    b. **ELINT** is intelligence derived from the interception and analysis of noncommunications emitters (e.g., radar). ELINT consists of two subcategories; operational electronic intelligence (OPELINT) and technical electronic intelligence (TECHELINT). **OPELINT** is concerned with operationally relevant information such as the location, movement, employment, tactics, and activity of foreign noncommunications emitters and their associated weapon systems. **TECHELINT** is concerned with the technical aspects of foreign noncommunications emitters such as signal characteristics, modes, functions, associations, capabilities, limitations, vulnerabilities, and technology levels.

    c. **FISINT** involves the technical analysis of data intercepted from foreign equipment and control systems such as telemetry, electronic interrogators, tracking/fusing/arming/firing command systems, and video data links.

4. Measurement and Signature Intelligence

    MASINT is information produced by quantitative and qualitative analysis of physical attributes of targets and events to characterize, locate, and identify them. MASINT exploits a variety of phenomenologies to support signature development and analysis, to perform technical analysis, and to detect, characterize, locate, and identify targets and events. MASINT is derived from specialized, technically-derived measurements of physical phenomenon intrinsic to an object or event and it includes the use of quantitative signatures to interpret the data. The measurement aspect of MASINT refers to actual measurements of parameters of an event or object such as the demonstrated flight profile and range of a cruise missile. Signatures are typically the products of multiple measurements collected over time and under varying circumstances. These signatures are used to develop target classification profiles and discrimination and reporting algorithms for operational surveillance and weapon systems. The technical data sources related to MASINT include:

    a. **EO data**—emitted or reflected energy across the visible/IR portion of the electromagnetic spectrum (ultraviolet, visible, near IR, and IR).

    b. **Radar data**—radar energy reflected (reradiated) from a target or objective.

    c. **Radio frequency data**—radio frequency/electromagnetic pulse emissions associated with nuclear testing, or other high energy events for the purpose of determining power levels, operating characteristics, and signatures of advanced technology weapons, power, and propulsion systems.

d. **Geophysical data**—phenomena transmitted through the Earth (ground, water, atmosphere) and man-made structures including emitted or reflected sounds, pressure waves, vibrations, and magnetic field or ionosphere disturbances. Subcategories include seismic intelligence, acoustic intelligence, and magnetic intelligence.

e. **Materials data**—gas, liquid, or solid samples, collected both by automatic equipment, such as air samplers, and directly by humans.

f. **Nuclear radiation data**—nuclear radiation and physical phenomena associated with nuclear weapons, processes, materials, devices, or facilities.

5. Open-Source Intelligence

OSINT is intelligence based on open source information that any member of the public can lawfully obtain by request, purchase, or observation. Examples of open sources include unofficial and draft documents, published and unpublished reference material, research, or 'cloud' databases, and web-based networking platforms or repositories. OSINT complements the other intelligence disciplines and can be used to fill gaps and provide accuracy and fidelity in classified information databases. OSINT is susceptible to manipulation and deception, and thus requires tradecraft and review during processing.

a. OSINT supports warnings, tips, and cues other intelligence disciplines, and provides the context for understanding classified information. It can also reduce large target sets, quickly filling information gaps, allowing the more efficient use of low-density technical and HUMINT assets. OSINT can be employed in a number of ways, including gauging population sentiment, discerning trends in foreign media, supporting sociocultural research and humanitarian assistance efforts, tracking scientific and technological developments, and enhancing foreign partnerships. OSINT products and sharing arrangements must be approved by JFC's FDO and conform to standing guidance. To facilitate OSINT sharing and review, the DIA's Open Source Collection Acquisition Requirements Management System is used to register collection requirements for IC action.

b. Like other types of intelligence, OSINT is susceptible to adversary deception attempts. Incorrect information may be deliberately planted in public sources. OSINT is also subject to source bias and inaccuracy. All-source intelligence should combine, compare, and analyze classified and open source material and attempt to cross-verify information obtained from different sources. In addition, OSINT requires tradecraft in the areas of research expertise and OPSEC for Internet-based activities.

c. **Gray Literature.** A non-doctrinal term used by various professions. Gray literature refers to a subset of open source information usually produced by research establishments that is neither published commercially nor universally accessible. Regardless of media, gray literature can include data or primary source information, academic reports and institutional data, informal personal or draft papers, unofficial or government exchanges.

d. **Intelink Sensitive But Unclassified (SBU).** Intelink SBU network, formerly known as open source information system, is a government-wide private network connecting members of the IC, DOD, DHS, law enforcement, and other information producers and consumers. Intelink-SBU is a community protected medium for the sharing of sensitive unclassified and commercially obtained information.

e. **Open-Source Acquisition.** The act of gaining possession of, or access to, open-source information synonymous with "open-source collection." The preferred term is acquisition because by definition, open sources are collected and disseminated by others. Open-source exploiters acquire previously collected and publicly available information second-hand. When traditional collection efforts fail, use of alternative collection is possible with OSINT. Fee for service OSINT collection, while sometimes costly, assists in filling gaps and meeting time requirements.

f. **Open-Source Collection.** See paragraph g, "Open-Source Acquisition." The OSINT functional manager for the IC is the CIA Director. Functional manager responsibilities are carried out by the Director, National Open Source Center. The DOD lead for OSINT is the Director, DIA.

g. **Open-Source Collection Acquisition Requirement Management System.** An IC web-enabled application for performing OSINT CRM. This is the IC collection management "program of record" for OSINT collection requirements.

6. Technical Intelligence

TECHINT is derived from the exploitation of foreign materiel and scientific information. TECHINT begins with the acquisition of a foreign piece of equipment or foreign scientific/technological information. The item or information is then exploited by specialized, multi-Service collection and analysis teams. These TECHINT teams assess the capabilities and vulnerabilities of captured military materiel and provide detailed assessments of foreign technological threat capabilities, limitations, and vulnerabilities.

a. TECHINT products are used by US weapons developers, countermeasure designers, tacticians, and operational forces to prevent technological surprise, neutralize an adversary's technological advantages, enhance force protection, and support the development and employment of effective countermeasures to newly identified adversary equipment. At the strategic level, the exploitation and interpretation of foreign weapon systems, materiel, and technologies is referred to as S&TI.

b. The DIA provides enhanced S&TI to CCDRs and their subordinates through the technical operational intelligence (TOPINT) program. TOPINT uses a closed loop system that integrates all Service and DIA S&T centers in a common effort. The TOPINT program provides timely collection, analysis, and dissemination of theater specific S&TI to CCDRs and their subordinates for planning, training, and executing joint operations.

c. Joint Captured Materiel Exploitation Center (JCMEC), managed by the DIA Joint Foreign Materiel Program Office, is the primary DOD contingency TECHINT capability. Activities of a JCMEC include recovery of foreign materiel and captured enemy equipment, and encompasses CCMD and national requirements. Subsequent exploitation of this materiel provides critical information on adversary strengths and weaknesses that may influence operational planning and force protection. The identification, recovery, in-theater analysis, and evacuation of this materiel is done by the JCMEC.

7. Counterintelligence

CI encompasses five functions (collection, analysis and production, investigations, operations, and functional services) conducted to identify, deceive, exploit, disrupt, or protect against espionage, other intelligence activities, sabotage, or assassinations conducted for or on behalf of foreign powers, organizations, or persons, or their agents, or international terrorist organizations or activities. CI is both offensive (adversary penetration and deception) and defensive (protection of vital US national security related information from being obtained or manipulated by an adversary's intelligence organizations, activities, and operations). This two-pronged approach forms a comprehensive CI strategy that feeds more effective CI functions. CI should be factored in whenever US intelligence or national security capabilities are deployed or when we are targeted by our adversaries. CI works closely with intelligence, security, infrastructure protection, and law enforcement to ensure an integrated approach to the protection of US forces, our intelligence and national assets; US research, development and technology; and the US economy.

CI is addressed in detail in JP 2-01.2, Counterintelligence and Human Intelligence Support to Joint Operations.

8. Applications

a. **I2.** I2 operations combine the synchronized application of biometrics, forensics, and DOMEX capabilities with intelligence and identity management processes to establish identity, affiliations and authorizations in order to deny anonymity to the adversary and protect US/PNs assets, facilities, and forces. The I2 operations process results in discovery of true identities, links identities to events, locations and networks, and reveals hostile intent. These outputs enable tasks, missions, and actions that span the range of military operations.

b. **DOMEX.** Captured documents and media, when processed and exploited, may provide valuable information such as adversary plans, intentions, locations, capabilities, and status. The category of "captured documents and media" includes all media capable of storing fixed information to include computer storage material. DOMEX may be conducted by any intelligence personnel with appropriate technical exploitation and language support.

c. **BEI.** Applied BEI supports the identification of individuals and their disposition at the point of encounter. Additionally, BEI and corresponding I2 products support the persistent identification and targeting of adversaries, which enables a range of military and civilian functions. While identity attributes (biographic, biologic, behavioral, and reputational) can be collected through intelligence disciplines, BEI provides additional layers of understanding and characterization of individuals and networks.

d. **FEI.** FEI results from the collection, processing, analysis, and interpretation of forensic material and data, as well as associated contextual data. This informs a decision maker's information needs with individualized information concerning events, ideology, and persons of interest.

Intentionally Blank

APPENDIX C
REFERENCES

The development of JP 2-0 is based upon the following primary references.

1. General

    a. Title 10, US Code, *Armed Forces.*

    b. Title 50, US Code, *War and National Defense.*

    c. The National Security Act of 1947.

    d. The Goldwater-Nichols Department of Defense Reorganization Act of 1986.

    e. The United Nations Participation Act of 1945.

    f. *National Policy and Procedures for the Disclosure of Classified Military Information to Foreign Governments and International Organizations (short title National Disclosure Policy-1).*

    g. Executive Order 12333, *United States Intelligence Activities.*

    h. Director Central Intelligence Directive 7/3, *Information Operations and Intelligence Community Related Activities.*

    i. National Decision Memorandum 119, *Disclosure of Classified US Military Information to Foreign Governments and International Organizations.*

2. Department of Defense

    a. DODD 3115.09, *DOD Intelligence Interrogations, Detainee Debriefings, and Tactical Questioning.*

    b. DODD 3600.01, *Information Operations (IO).*

    c. DODD 5100.01, *Functions of the Department of Defense and its Major Components.*

    d. DODD 5230.11, *Disclosure of Classified Military Information to Foreign Governments and International Organizations.*

    e. DODD 5240.01, *DOD Intelligence Activities.*

    f. DODD 8521.01E, *Department of Defense Biometrics.*

    g. DOD 5240.1-R, *Procedures Governing the Activities of DOD Intelligence Components That Affect United States Persons.*

    h. DOD Instruction 3305.07, *Joint Reserve Intelligence Program (JRIP).*

i. DOD Instruction 3305.8, *Management and Administration of the Joint Reserve Intelligence Program (JRIP)*.

3. Chairman of the Joint Chiefs of Staff

a. CJCS Message DTG 031640Z April 06, Joint Intelligence Operations Center (JIOC) Execute Order, Mod 3 DTG 040001Z October 11.

b. CJCSI 3110.02, *Intelligence Planning Objectives, Guidance, and Tasks*.

c. CJCSI 3150.25E, *Joint Lessons Learned Program*.

d. CJCSI 3370.01, *Target Development Standards*.

e. CJCSI 5120.02C, *Joint Doctrine Development System*.

f. CJCSM 3130.03, *Adaptive Planning and Execution Planning Formats and Guidance*.

g. CJCSM 3314.01A, *Intelligence Planning*.

h. CJCSM 3500.04F, *Universal Joint Task Manual*.

i. JP 1, *Doctrine for the Armed Forces of the United States*.

j. JP 1-0, *Joint Personnel Support*.

k. JP 1-02, *Department of Defense Dictionary of Military and Associated Terms*.

l. JP 2-01, *Joint and National Intelligence Support to Military Operations*.

m. JP 2-01.2, *Counterintelligence and Human Intelligence Support to Joint Operations*.

n. JP 2-01.3, *Joint Intelligence Preparation of the Operational Environment*.

o. JP 2-03, *Geospatial Intelligence in Joint Operations*.

p. JP 3-0, *Joint Operations*.

q. JP 3-08, *Interorganizational Coordination During Joint Operations*.

r. JP 3-09, *Joint Fire Support*.

s. JP 3-13, *Information Operations*.

t. JP 3-16, *Multinational Operations*.

u. JP 3-27, *Homeland Defense*.

v. JP 3-28, *Defense Support of Civil Authorities*.

w. JP 3-33, *Joint Task Force Headquarters.*

x. JP 3-40, *Countering Weapons of Mass Destruction.*

y. JP 3-60, *Joint Targeting.*

z. JP 5-0, *Joint Operation Planning.*

aa. JP 6-0, *Joint Communications System.*

Intentionally Blank

APPENDIX D
ADMINISTRATIVE INSTRUCTIONS

1. User Comments

Users in the field are highly encouraged to submit comments on this publication to: Joint Staff J-7, Deputy Director, Joint Education and Doctrine, ATTN: Joint Doctrine Analysis Division, 116 Lake View Parkway, Suffolk, VA 23435-2697. These comments should address content (accuracy, usefulness, consistency, and organization), writing, and appearance.

2. Authorship

The lead agent and Joint Staff doctrine sponsor for this publication is the Director for Intelligence (J-2).

3. Supersession

This publication supersedes JP 2-0, 22 June 2007, *Joint Intelligence.*

4. Change Recommendations

a. Recommendations for urgent changes to this publication should be submitted:

TO: JOINT STAFF WASHINGTON DC//J7-JE&D//

b. Routine changes should be submitted electronically to the Deputy Director, Joint Education and Doctrine, ATTN: Joint Doctrine Analysis Division, 116 Lake View Parkway, Suffolk, VA 23435-2697, and info the lead agent and the Director for Joint Force Development, J-7/JE&D.

c. When a Joint Staff directorate submits a proposal to the CJCS that would change source document information reflected in this publication, that directorate will include a proposed change to this publication as an enclosure to its proposal. The Services and other organizations are requested to notify the Joint Staff J-7 when changes to source documents reflected in this publication are initiated.

5. Distribution of Publications

Local reproduction is authorized, and access to unclassified publications is unrestricted. However, access to and reproduction authorization for classified JPs must be IAW DOD Manual 5200.01, Volume 1, *DOD Information Security Program: Overview, Classification, and Declassification,* and DOD Manual 5200.01, Volume 3, *DOD Information Security Program: Protection of Classified Information.*

6. Distribution of Electronic Publications

a. Joint Staff J-7 will not print copies of JPs for distribution. Electronic versions are available on JDEIS at https://jdeis.js.mil (NIPRNET) and http://jdeis.js.smil.mil (SIPRNET), and on the JEL at http://www.dtic.mil/doctrine (NIPRNET).

b. Only approved JPs are releasable outside the combatant commands, Services, and Joint Staff. Release of any classified JP to foreign governments or foreign nationals must be requested through the local embassy (Defense Attaché Office) to DIA, Defense Foreign Liaison/IE-3, 200 MacDill Blvd., Joint Base Anacostia-Bolling, Washington, DC 20340-5100.

c. JEL CD-ROM. Upon request of a joint doctrine development community member, the Joint Staff J-7 will produce and deliver one CD-ROM with current JPs. This JEL CD-ROM will be updated not less than semi-annually and when received can be locally reproduced for use within the combatant commands, Services, and combat support agencies.

GLOSSARY
PART I—ABBREVIATIONS AND ACRONYMS

AOI	area of interest
AOR	area of responsibility
APEX	Adaptive Planning and Execution
BDA	battle damage assessment
BEI	biometrics-enabled intelligence
CCDR	combatant commander
CCIR	commander's critical information requirement
CCMD	combatant command
CENTRIXS	Combined Enterprise Regional Information Exchange System
CI	counterintelligence
CIA	Central Intelligence Agency
CJCS	Chairman of the Joint Chiefs of Staff
CJCSI	Chairman of the Joint Chiefs of Staff instruction
CJCSM	Chairman of the Joint Chiefs of Staff manual
CMA	collection management authority
CMO	civil-military operations
COA	course of action
COG	center of gravity
COM	collection operations management
COMINT	communications intelligence
CONOPS	concept of operations
COP	common operational picture
CRM	collection requirements management
CSA	combat support agency
CSS	Central Security Service (NSA)
DHS	Department of Homeland Security
DIA	Defense Intelligence Agency
DIAP	Defense Intelligence Analysis Program
DNI	Director of National Intelligence
DOD	Department of Defense
DODD	Department of Defense directive
DODIN	Department of Defense information networks
DOE	Department of Energy
DOMEX	document and media exploitation
DOS	Department of State
DSCA	defense support of civil authorities
DTA	dynamic threat assessment

EEI	essential element of information
ELINT	electronic intelligence
EO	electro-optical
FBI	Federal Bureau of Investigation (DOJ)
FDO	foreign disclosure officer
FEI	forensic-enabled intelligence
FFIR	friendly force information requirement
FISINT	foreign instrumentation signals intelligence
GEOINT	geospatial intelligence
GFM	global force management
GMI	general military intelligence
HSI	hyperspectral imagery
HUMINT	human intelligence
HVT	high-value target
I2	identity intelligence
IAA	incident awareness and assessment
IC	intelligence community
ICW	in coordination with
IGO	intergovernmental organization
IMINT	imagery intelligence
IO	information operations
IOII	information operations intelligence integration
IP	intelligence planning
IPR	in-progress review
IPT	intelligence planning team
IR	infrared
IRC	information-related capability
ISR	intelligence, surveillance, and reconnaissance
J-2	intelligence directorate of a joint staff
J-2X	joint force counterintelligence and human intelligence staff element
J-3	operations directorate of a joint staff
J-5	plans directorate of a joint staff
J-6	communications system directorate of a joint staff
JCMB	joint collection management board
JCMEC	Joint Captured Materiel Exploitation Center (DIA)
JCS	Joint Chiefs of Staff
JDISS	joint deployable intelligence support system
JFC	joint force commander
JFCC-ISR	Joint Functional Component Command for Intelligence, Surveillance, and Reconnaissance (USSTRATCOM)

JIACG	joint interagency coordination group
JIOC	joint intelligence operations center
JIPOE	joint intelligence preparation of the operational environment
JISE	joint intelligence support element
JLLP	Joint Lessons Learned Program
JOPP	joint operation planning process
JP	joint publication
JPG	joint planning group
JRC	joint reconnaissance center
JRIC	joint reserve intelligence center
JRIP	Joint Reserve Intelligence Program
JTF	joint task force
JTL	joint target list
JWICS	Joint Worldwide Intelligence Communications System
LOE	line of effort
MASINT	measurement and signature intelligence
MEA	munitions effectiveness assessment
MEDINT	medical intelligence
MIB	Military Intelligence Board
MIP	military intelligence program
MOE	measure of effectiveness
MOP	measure of performance
MSI	multispectral imagery
NATO	North Atlantic Treaty Organization
NDP	national disclosure policy
NGA	National Geospatial-Intelligence Agency
NGO	nongovernmental organization
NIP	National Intelligence Program
NISP	national intelligence support plan
NJOIC	National Joint Operations and Intelligence Center
NMCC	National Military Command Center
NRO	National Reconnaissance Office
NSA	National Security Agency
NSL	no-strike list
ODNI	Office of the Director of National Intelligence
OE	operational environment
OPELINT	operational electronic intelligence
OPLAN	operation plan
OPORD	operation order
OPSEC	operations security
OSD	Office of the Secretary of Defense
OSINT	open-source intelligence

PED	processing, exploitation, and dissemination
PIR	priority intelligence requirement
PMESII	political, military, economic, social, information, and infrastructure
PN	partner nation
RATE	refine, adapt, terminate, execute
RFF	request for forces
RFI	request for information
RTL	restricted target list
S&T	scientific and technical
S&TI	scientific and technical intelligence
SBU	sensitive but unclassified
SCA	sociocultural analysis
SCI	sensitive compartmented information
SecDef	Secretary of Defense
SIGINT	signals intelligence
SIR	specific information requirement
SME	subject matter expert
SOF	special operations forces
TECHELINT	technical electronic intelligence
TECHINT	technical intelligence
TIA	theater intelligence assessment
TOPINT	technical operational intelligence
TSA	target system analysis
USCG	United States Coast Guard
USD(I)	Under Secretary of Defense for Intelligence
USSTRATCOM	United States Strategic Command
WMD	weapons of mass destruction

acoustic intelligence. Intelligence derived from the collection and processing of acoustic phenomena. Also called **ACINT.** (JP 1-02. SOURCE: JP 2-0)

all-source intelligence. 1. Intelligence products and/or organizations and activities that incorporate all sources of information in the production of finished intelligence. 2. In intelligence collection, a phrase that indicates that in the satisfaction of intelligence requirements, all collection, processing, exploitation, and reporting systems and resources are identified for possible use and those most capable are tasked. (Approved for incorporation into JP 1-02.)

application. 1. The system or problem to which a computer is applied. 2. In the intelligence context, the direct extraction and tailoring of information from an existing foundation of intelligence and near real time reporting. (Approved for incorporation into JP 1-02.)

biometric. None. (Approved for removal from JP 1-02.)

biometrics. The process of recognizing an individual based on measurable anatomical, physiological, and behavioral characteristics. (JP 1-02. SOURCE: JP 2-0)

biometrics-enabled intelligence. The intelligence derived from the processing of biologic identity data and other all-source for information concerning persons of interest. Also called **BEI.** (Approved for inclusion in JP 1-02.)

burn notice. None. (Approved for removal from JP 1-02.)

case. None. (Approved for removal from JP 1-02.)

collate. None. (Approved for removal from JP 1-02.)

collection management. In intelligence usage, the process of converting intelligence requirements into collection requirements, establishing priorities, tasking or coordinating with appropriate collection sources or agencies, monitoring results, and retasking, as required. (JP 1-02. SOURCE: JP 2-0)

collection operations management. The authoritative direction, scheduling, and control of specific collection operations and associated processing, exploitation, and reporting resources. Also called **COM.** (JP 1-02. SOURCE: JP 2-0)

collection plan. A systematic scheme to optimize the employment of all available collection capabilities and associated processing, exploitation, and dissemination resources to satisfy specific information requirements. (Approved for incorporation into JP 1-02.)

collection planning. A continuous process that coordinates and integrates the efforts of all collection units and agencies. (JP 1-02. SOURCE: JP 2-0)

collection posture. The current status of collection assets and resources to satisfy identified information requirements. (Approved for inclusion in JP 1-02.)

collection requirement. A valid need to close a specific gap in intelligence holdings in direct response to a request for information. (Approved for incorporation into JP 1-02.)

collection requirements management. The authoritative development and control of collection, processing, exploitation, and/or reporting requirements that normally result in either the direct tasking of requirements to units over which the commander has authority, or the generation of tasking requests to collection management authorities at a higher, lower, or lateral echelon to accomplish the collection mission. Also called **CRM.** (Approved for incorporation into JP 1-02.)

collection strategy. An analytical approach used by collection managers to determine which intelligence disciplines can be applied to satisfy information requirements. (Approved for inclusion in JP 1-02.)

combat intelligence. None. (Approved for removal from JP 1-02.)

communications intelligence. Technical information and intelligence derived from foreign communications by other than the intended recipients. Also called **COMINT.** (JP 1-02. SOURCE: JP 2-0)

concept of intelligence operations. Within the Department of Defense, a verbal or graphic statement, in broad outline, of an intelligence directorate's assumptions or intent in regard to intelligence support of an operation or series of operations. (Approved for incorporation into JP 1-02.)

confirmation of information (intelligence). None. (Approved for removal from JP 1-02.)

critical information. Specific facts about friendly intentions, capabilities, and activities needed by adversaries for them to plan and act effectively so as to guarantee failure or unacceptable consequences for friendly mission accomplishment. Also called **CRITIC.** (Approved for incorporation into JP 1-02.)

critical intelligence. Intelligence that is crucial and requires the immediate attention of the commander. (Approved for incorporation into JP 1-02.)

current intelligence. None. (Approved for removal from JP 1-02.)

database. None. (Approved for removal from JP 1-02.)

declassification. None. (Approved for removal from JP 1-02.)

Department of Defense Intelligence Information System. The combination of Department of Defense personnel, procedures, equipment, computer programs, and supporting communications that support the timely and comprehensive preparation and presentation of intelligence and information to military commanders and national-level decision makers. Also called **DODIIS.** (JP 1-02. SOURCE: JP 2-0)

Department of Defense Intelligence Information System Enterprise. None. (Approved for removal from JP 1-02.)

Department of Defense intelligence production. None. (Approved for removal from JP 1-02.)

direction. None. (Approved for removal from JP 1-02.)

dynamic threat assessment. An intelligence assessment developed by the Defense Intelligence Agency that details the threat, capabilities, and intentions of adversaries in each of the priority plans in the Joint Strategic Capabilities Plan. Also called **DTA.** (Approved for incorporation into JP 1-02.)

electro-optical intelligence. None. (Approved for removal from JP 1-02.)

elicitation. In intelligence usage, the acquisition of information from a person or group in a manner that does not disclose the intent of the interview or conversation. (Approved for replacement of "elicitation (intelligence)" and its definition in JP 1-02.)

essential elements of information. The most critical information requirements regarding the adversary and the environment needed by the commander by a particular time to relate with other available information and intelligence in order to assist in reaching a logical decision. Also called **EEIs.** (JP 1-02. SOURCE: JP 2-0)

estimative intelligence. Intelligence that identifies, describes, and forecasts adversary capabilities and the implications for planning and executing military operations. (JP 1-02. SOURCE: JP 2-0)

foreign intelligence. Information relating to capabilities, intentions, or activities of foreign governments or elements thereof, foreign organizations, or foreign persons, or international terrorist activities. Also called **FI.** (Approved for incorporation into JP 1-02.)

forensic-enabled intelligence. The intelligence resulting from the integration of scientifically examined materials and other information to establish full characterization, attribution, and the linkage of events, locations, items, signatures, nefarious intent, and persons of interest. Also called **FEI.** (Approved for inclusion in JP 1-02.)

fusion. In intelligence usage, the process of managing information to conduct all-source analysis and derive a complete assessment of activity. (Approved for incorporation into JP 1-02.)

general military intelligence. Intelligence concerning the military capabilities of foreign countries or organizations, or topics affecting potential United States or multinational military operations. Also called **GMI.** (Approved for incorporation into JP 1-02.)

human factors. The physical, cultural, psychological, and behavioral attributes of an individual or group that influence perceptions, understanding, and interactions. (Approved for incorporation into JP 1-02.)

human intelligence. A category of intelligence derived from information collected and provided by human sources. Also called **HUMINT.** (JP 1-02. SOURCE: JP 2-0)

identity intelligence. The intelligence resulting from the processing of identity attributes concerning individuals, groups, networks, or populations of interest. Also called **I2.** (Approved for inclusion in JP 1-02.)

indications. In intelligence usage, information in various degrees of evaluation, all of which bear on the intention of a potential enemy to adopt or reject a course of action. (JP 1-02. SOURCE: JP 2-0)

indications and warning. None. (Approved for removal from JP 1-02.)

indicator. In intelligence usage, an item of information which reflects the intention or capability of an adversary to adopt or reject a course of action. (JP 1-02. SOURCE: JP 2-0)

information requirements. In intelligence usage, those items of information regarding the adversary and other relevant aspects of the operational environment that need to be collected and processed in order to meet the intelligence requirements of a commander. Also called **IR.** (Approved for incorporation into JP 1-02.)

intelligence. 1. The product resulting from the collection, processing, integration, evaluation, analysis, and interpretation of available information concerning foreign nations, hostile or potentially hostile forces or elements, or areas of actual or potential operations. 2. The activities that result in the product. 3. The organizations engaged in such activities. (Approved for incorporation into JP 1-02.)

intelligence asset. Any resource utilized by an intelligence organization for an operational support role. (Approved for replacement of "asset (intelligence)" and its definition in JP 1-02.)

intelligence community. All departments or agencies of a government that are concerned with intelligence activity, either in an oversight, managerial, support, or participatory role. Also called **IC.** (Approved for incorporation into JP 1-02 with JP 2-0 as the source JP.)

intelligence discipline. A well-defined area of intelligence planning, collection, processing, exploitation, analysis, and reporting using a specific category of technical or human resources. (Approved for incorporation into JP 1-02.)

intelligence estimate. The appraisal, expressed in writing or orally, of available intelligence relating to a specific situation or condition with a view to determining the courses of action open to the enemy or adversary and the order of probability of their adoption. (JP 1-02. SOURCE: JP 2-0)

intelligence planning. The intelligence component of the Adaptive Planning and Execution system, which coordinates and integrates all available Defense Intelligence Enterprise capabilities to meet combatant commander intelligence requirements. Also called **IP.** (Approved for inclusion in JP 1-02.)

intelligence production. The integration, evaluation, analysis, and interpretation of information from single or multiple sources into finished intelligence for known or anticipated military and related national security consumer requirements. (Approved for inclusion in JP 1-02.)

intelligence requirement. 1. Any subject, general or specific, upon which there is a need for the collection of information, or the production of intelligence. 2. A requirement for intelligence to fill a gap in the command's knowledge or understanding of the operational environment or threat forces. Also called **IR.** (Approved for incorporation into JP 1-02.)

intelligence source. The means or system that can be used to observe and record information relating to the condition, situation, or activities of a targeted location, organization, or individual. (Approved for incorporation into JP 1-02.)

joint deployable intelligence support system. A transportable workstation and communications suite that electronically extends a joint intelligence center to a joint task force or other tactical user. Also called **JDISS.** (JP 1-02. SOURCE: JP 2-0)

joint intelligence. Intelligence produced by elements of more than one Service of the same nation. (JP 1-02. SOURCE: JP 2-0)

joint intelligence architecture. A dynamic, flexible structure that consists of the Defense Joint Intelligence Operations Center, combatant command joint intelligence operations centers, and subordinate joint task force intelligence operations centers or joint intelligence support elements to provide national, theater, and tactical commanders with the full range of intelligence required for planning and conducting operations. (Approved for incorporation into JP 1-02.)

joint intelligence operations center. An interdependent, operational intelligence organization at the Department of Defense, combatant command, or joint task force (if established) level, that is integrated with national intelligence centers, and capable of accessing all sources of intelligence impacting military operations planning, execution, and assessment. Also called **JIOC.** (JP 1-02. SOURCE: JP 2-0)

Joint Worldwide Intelligence Communications System. The sensitive compartmented information portion of the Defense Information Systems Network, which incorporates advanced networking technologies that permit point-to-point or multipoint information exchange involving voice, text, graphics, data, and video teleconferencing. Also called **JWICS.** (Approved for incorporation into JP 1-02.)

laser intelligence. None. (Approved for removal from JP 1-02.)

measurement and signature intelligence. Information produced by quantitative and qualitative analysis of physical attributes of targets and events to characterize, locate, and identify targets and events, and derived from specialized, technically derived measurements of physical phenomenon intrinsic to an object or event. Also called **MASINT.** (Approved for incorporation into JP 1-02.)

Military Intelligence Board. A decision-making forum which formulates Department of Defense intelligence policy and programming priorities. Also called **MIB.** (JP 1-02. SOURCE: JP 2-0)

national intelligence support team. None. (Approved for removal from JP 1-02.)

National Reconnaissance Office. None. (Approved for removal from JP 1-02.)

nuclear intelligence. None. (Approved for removal from JP 1-02.)

open-source information. Information that any member of the public could lawfully obtain by request or observation as well as other unclassified information that has limited public distribution or access. (Approved for inclusion in JP 1-02.)

open-source intelligence. Relevant information derived from the systematic collection, processing, and analysis of publicly available information in response to known or anticipated intelligence requirements. Also called **OSINT.** (Approved for incorporation into JP 1-02.)

operational architecture. None. (Approved for removal from JP 1-02.)

operational intelligence. Intelligence that is required for planning and conducting campaigns and major operations to accomplish strategic objectives within theaters or operational areas. (JP 1-02. SOURCE: JP 2-0)

persistent surveillance. None. (Approved for removal from JP 1-02.)

processing. A system of operations designed to convert raw data into useful information. (JP 1-02. SOURCE: JP 2-0)

production requirement. An intelligence requirement that cannot be met by current analytical products resulting in tasking to produce a new product that can meet this intelligence requirement. Also called **PR.** (Approved for inclusion in JP 1-02.)

radar intelligence. None. (Approved for removal from JP 1-02.)

reconnaissance. A mission undertaken to obtain, by visual observation or other detection methods, information about the activities and resources of an enemy or adversary, or to secure data concerning the meteorological, hydrographic, or geographic characteristics of a particular area. Also called **RECON.** (JP 1-02. SOURCE: JP 2-0)

red team. An organizational element comprised of trained and educated members that provide an independent capability to fully explore alternatives in plans and operations in the context of the operational environment and from the perspective of adversaries and others. (JP 1-02. SOURCE: JP 2-0)

request for information. 1. Any specific time-sensitive ad hoc requirement for intelligence information or products to support an ongoing crisis or operation not necessarily related to standing requirements or scheduled intelligence production. 2. A term used by the National Security Agency/Central Security Service to state ad hoc signals intelligence requirements. Also called **RFI.** (Approved for incorporation into JP 1-02.)

security. 1. Measures taken by a military unit, activity, or installation to protect itself against all acts designed to, or which may, impair its effectiveness. (JP 3-10) 2. A condition that results from the establishment and maintenance of protective measures that ensure a state of inviolability from hostile acts or influences. (JP 3-10) 3. With respect to classified matter, the condition that prevents unauthorized persons from having access to official information that is safeguarded in the interests of national security. (JP 1-02. SOURCE: JP 2-0)

signals intelligence. 1. A category of intelligence comprising either individually or in combination all communications intelligence, electronic intelligence, and foreign instrumentation signals intelligence, however transmitted. 2. Intelligence derived from communications, electronic, and foreign instrumentation signals. Also called **SIGINT.** (JP 1-02. SOURCE: JP 2-0)

sociocultural analysis. The analysis of adversaries and other relevant actors that integrates concepts, knowledge, and understanding of societies, populations, and other groups of people, including their activities, relationships, and perspectives across time and space at varying scales. Also called **SCA.** (Approved for inclusion in JP 1-02.)

synchronization. 1. The arrangement of military actions in time, space, and purpose to produce maximum relative combat power at a decisive place and time. 2. In the intelligence context, application of intelligence sources and methods in concert with the operation plan to answer intelligence requirements in time to influence the decisions they support. (Approved for incorporation into JP 1-02.)

synthesis. In intelligence usage, the examining and combining of processed information with other information and intelligence for final interpretation. (Approved for incorporation into JP 1-02 with JP 2-0 as the source JP.)

tear line. A physical line on an intelligence message or document separating categories of information that have been approved for foreign disclosure and release. (Approved for incorporation into JP 1-02.)

technical architecture. None. (Approved for removal from JP 1-02.)

technical intelligence. Intelligence derived from the collection, processing, analysis, and exploitation of data and information pertaining to foreign equipment and materiel for the purposes of preventing technological surprise, assessing foreign scientific and technical capabilities, and developing countermeasures designed to neutralize an adversary's technological advantages. Also called **TECHINT.** (JP 1-02. SOURCE: JP 2-0)

technical operational intelligence. None. (Approved for removal from JP 1-02.)

warning intelligence. Those intelligence activities intended to detect and report time-sensitive intelligence information on foreign developments that forewarn of hostile actions or intention against United States entities, partners, or interests. (Approved for inclusion in JP 1-02.)

JOINT DOCTRINE PUBLICATIONS HIERARCHY

JP 1
JOINT DOCTRINE
JP 1-0
PERSONNEL
JP 2-0
INTELLIGENCE
JP 3-0
OPERATIONS
JP 4-0
LOGISTICS
JP 5-0
PLANS
JP 6-0
COMMUNICATIONS SYSTEM

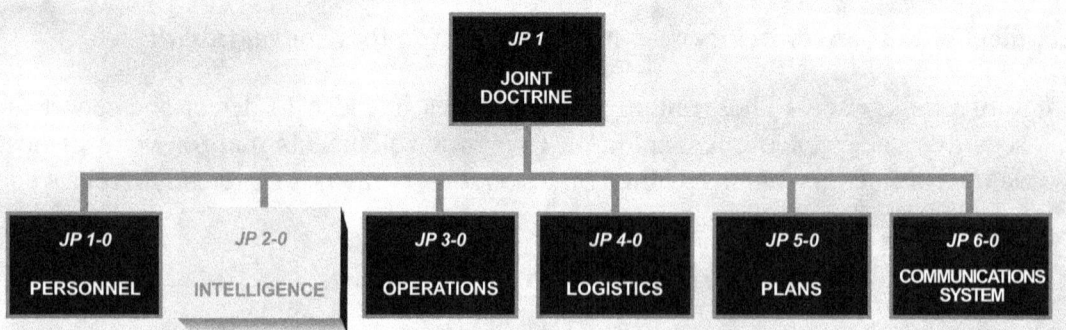

All joint publications are organized into a comprehensive hierarchy as shown in the chart above. **Joint Publication (JP) 2-0** is in the **Intelligence** series of joint doctrine publications. The diagram below illustrates an overview of the development process:

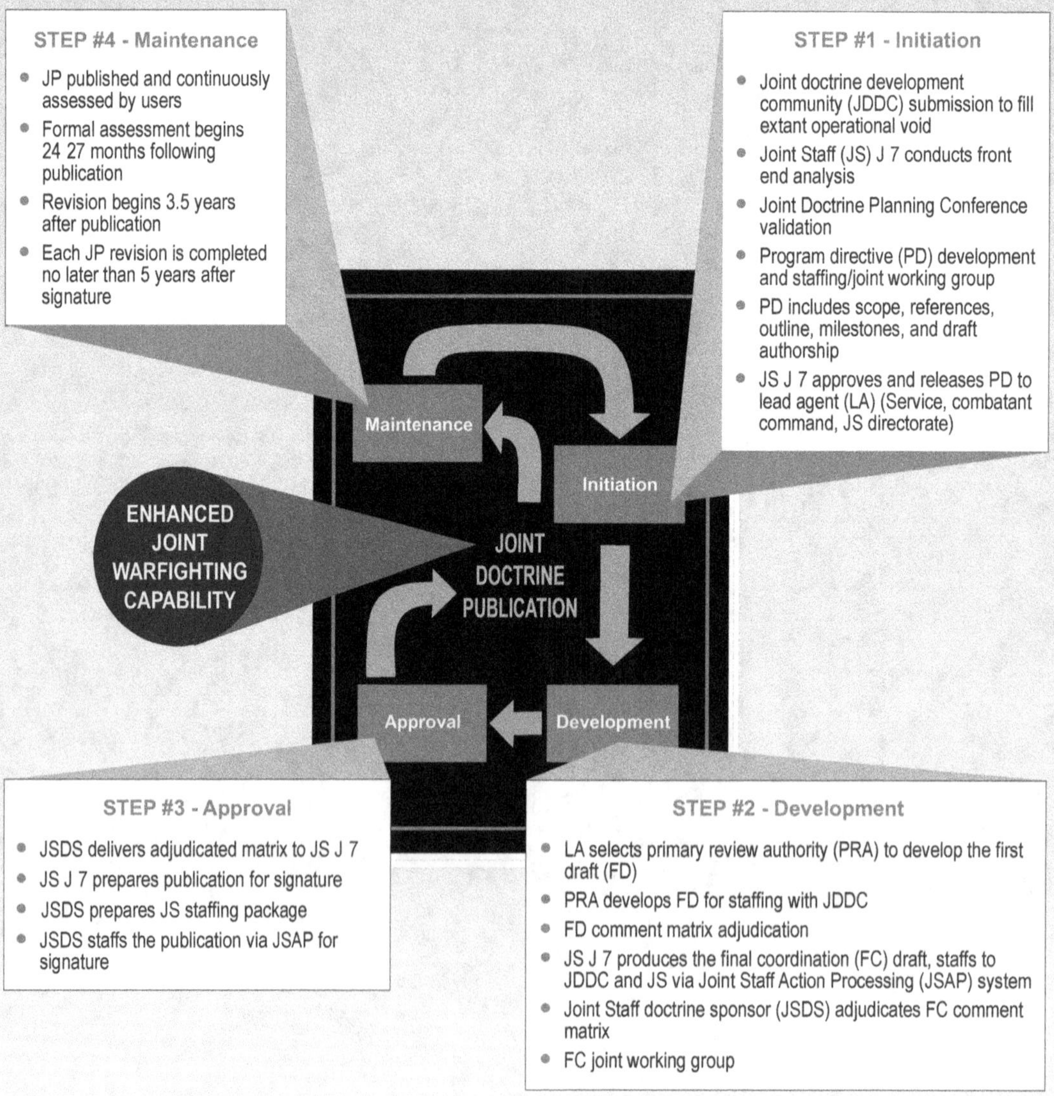

STEP #4 - Maintenance
JP published and continuously assessed by users
Formal assessment begins 24 27 months following publication
Revision begins 3.5 years after publication
Each JP revision is completed no later than 5 years after signature
STEP #1 - Initiation
Joint doctrine development community (JDDC) submission to fill extant operational void
Joint Staff (JS) J 7 conducts front end analysis
Joint Doctrine Planning Conference validation
Program directive (PD) development and staffing/joint working group
PD includes scope, references, outline, milestones, and draft authorship
JS J 7 approves and releases PD to lead agent (LA) (Service, combatant command, JS directorate)
Maintenance
Initiation
ENHANCED JOINT WARFIGHTING CAPABILITY
JOINT DOCTRINE PUBLICATION
Approval
Development
STEP #3 - Approval
JSDS delivers adjudicated matrix to JS J 7
JS J 7 prepares publication for signature
JSDS prepares JS staffing package
JSDS staffs the publication via JSAP for signature
STEP #2 - Development
LA selects primary review authority (PRA) to develop the first draft (FD)
PRA develops FD for staffing with JDDC
FD comment matrix adjudication
JS J 7 produces the final coordination (FC) draft, staffs to JDDC and JS via Joint Staff Action Processing (JSAP) system
Joint Staff doctrine sponsor (JSDS) adjudicates FC comment matrix
FC joint working group

www.ingramcontent.com/pod-product-compliance
Lightning Source LLC
Chambersburg PA
CBHW081829280526

45789CB00007B/2393